www. wadsworth.com

www.wadsworth.com is the World Wide Web site
for Wadsworth and is your direct source to dozens
of online resources.

At *www.wadsworth.com* you can find out about
supplements, demonstration software, and
student resources. You can also send email to
many of our authors and preview new
publications and exciting new technologies.

www.wadsworth.com
Changing the way the world learns®

The Elements of Social Scientific Thinking Eighth Edition

Kenneth Hoover
Western Washington University

Todd Donovan
Western Washington University

THOMSON
*—
WADSWORTH

Australia • Canada • Mexico • Singapore • Spain
United Kingdom • United States

THOMSON

WADSWORTH

Publisher: *Clark Baxter*
Executive Editor: *David Tatom*
Assistant Editor: *Amy McGaughey*
Editorial Assistant: *Dianna Long*
Technology Project Manager: M*elinda Newfarmer*
Marketing Manager: *Janise Fry*
Marketing Assistant: *Mary Ho*
Advertising Project Manager: *Nathaniel Bergson-Michelson*
Project Manager, Editorial Production: *Matt Ballantyne*
Print/Media Buyer: *Kris Waller*

Permissions Editor: *Joohee Lee*
Production Service: *Shepherd, Inc.*
Text Designer: *Lisa Delgado*
Copy Editor: *Cheryl Ferguson*
Cover Designer: *Brian Salisbury*
Cover Image: *AL 3, by László Moholy-Nagy. Courtesy of the Norton Simon Museum, The Blue Four Galka Scheyer Collection, 1953. Reprinted with permission of the Artists Rights Society.*
Compositor: *Shepherd, Inc.*
Text and Cover Printer: *Webcom, Limited*

Printed in Canada
1 2 3 4 5 6 7 07 06 05 04 03

For more information about our products, contact us at:
Thomson Learning Academic Resource Center
1-800-423-0563
For permission to use material from this text, contact us by:
Phone: 1-800-730-2214
Fax: 1-800-730-2215
Web: http://www.thomsonrights.com

Library of Congress Control Number: 2003108365
ISBN 0-534-61411-6

Wadsworth/Thomson Learning
10 Davis Drive
Belmont, CA 94002-3098
USA

Asia
Thomson Learning
5 Shenton Way #01-01
UIC Building
Singapore 068808

Australia/New Zealand
Thomson Learning
102 Dodds Street
Southbank, Victoria 3006
Australia

Canada
Nelson
1120 Birchmount Road
Toronto, Ontario MIK 5G4
Canada

Europe/Middle East/Africa
Thomson Learning
High Holborn House
50/51 Bedford Row
London WCIR 4LR
United Kingdom

Spain/Portugal
Paraninfo
Calle/Magallanes, 25
28015 Madrid, Spain

To our families

Contents

Preface

This little book is not very complicated. It is, rather, an initiation into social science intended for those who use the results of social science research and for those taking their first steps as researchers. Where do concepts come from? What is a variable? Why bother with scientific thinking? How is a hypothesis different from other statements about reality? How is it similar? These and other fundamental questions are dealt with here.

Our intent has been to help readers see through some false images of social science and to say enough to make the first steps in research possible for them, while leaving to more detailed and specialized sources the elaboration of the technicalities of research operations. Throughout, the emphasis is on reality testing as a process by which we can know what to make of the world. This presentation of science is not a narrow one—we encourage the reader to be scientific in daily thought as well as in the specific application of social scientific methods.

Changes in the Eighth Edition

This book had its origins more than a quarter of a century ago when Kenneth Hoover, a young political theorist, reflected upon his own education in the social sciences and tried to make sense of the key concepts and techniques so that they could be explained to new generations of undergraduates. The author was initially repelled by quantitative analysis and the scientific approach to politics. However, he came to learn how it could contribute to answering what Hanna Pitkin identifies as the theorist's most basic question: What can be done to improve the human condition—and what matters are beyond our ability to change?[1] Perhaps the longevity of the book owes something to its origins outside the field of methodology, and to an interest in making the tools of social science available to students interested in social change.

In this eighth edition of *The Elements of Social Scientific Thinking*, we have continued the partnership between Kenneth Hoover, a theorist, and Todd Donovan, a behavioral analyst, who did the principal work on this revision. Donovan's work uses a variety of survey and statistical techniques to focus on how citizens are able to participate in a mass democracy. We keep working at situating scientific knowledge with respect to other forms of "knowing" so that students will see through some of the stereotypes that have clouded this discussion. The central lesson remains the same: Science is about the reduction of uncertainty in a world of phenomena that are only partially knowable through observation. The point of this book is to see what observation can accomplish.

We have also continued the emphasis on straightforward explanation. Numerous minor changes have been made; however, the increasing sophistication of statistical tools, and the pervasiveness of computers that have increased access to these tools, have necessitated some additions to the sections on research techniques. We have replaced one appendix in order to include examples of research questions that may be of wider interest to sociologists, political scientists, and other social scientists. The new Appendix A provides an introduction to a discussion of America's declining "social capital" in order to illustrate how scholars have approached the changing relationship of community involvement and political participation.

Our conviction is that the debate between social scientists who quantify and those who don't (and between so-called positivists and antipositivists) has served the valuable purpose of broadening the array of tools and perspectives available to social scientists. This debate has also absorbed a huge amount of energy and enterprise that would now be better directed at making constructive use of all the techniques of social analysis. If nothing else, it is evident that no one approach holds all the answers, and that every approach has its particular pitfalls and openings to prejudice. Choosing the appropriate methodology, or combination of methodologies, is the critical consideration.

While social scientists have been occupied with these debates, society's problems seem to have grown more complex and difficult to resolve. If careful observation is critical in understanding these problems, then social science has a key role to play.

The classic rules of scientific inquiry provide a framework for resolving conflicts over that most contentious matter, the truth, even between people who don't particularly like each other. Useful ideas from all sources of insight badly need to be tested through systematic analysis so that conflicting points of view can be resolved into productive forms of action.

How to Read This Book

Most books are meant to be read straight through. For many readers, that will be the best approach for this book. However, the reader should be aware that each chapter surveys social scientific thinking at a different level. For that reason, there can be various points of access to the book depending on the reader's needs. The first chapter, "Thinking Scientifically," sets social science in the general context of the ways in which people try to answer questions about the world around them. Chapter Two, "The Elements of Science," develops the basic outline of the scientific method by discussing concepts, variables, measurements, hypotheses, and theory.

For those faced with the immediate task of doing or understanding research, Chapter Three, "Strategies," may be a good place to begin because it deals directly with the nuts and bolts of scientific inquiry. Chapter Four, "Refinements," presumes a basic understanding of the scientific method explained in Chapter Two and provides additional research tools. Chapter Five, "Measuring Variables and Relationships," is devoted to the art and science of measurement. Chapter Six, "Reflections: Back to the Roots," should be read, we think, by those who use the book for any purpose. The point of this concluding chapter is to place scientific understanding in perspective and to suggest generally where humility is advisable and achievement possible.

For convenience of access and review, each chapter begins with an outline of the topics covered and ends with a list of the major concepts introduced, in their order of appearance.

In Appendix A, an article entitled "Tuning in and Tuning Out: The Strange Disappearance of Social Capital in America" by Robert Putnam, is reprinted in condensed form. The article is cited frequently in the text; those who need a good model for generating research questions will want to consider it carefully. Appendix B consists of an article entitled "Minority Representation under Cumulative and Limited Voting," by David Brockington, Todd Donovan, Shaun Bowler, and Robert Brischetto. Appendix B is relevant only to the section on regression analysis in Chapter Five.

We invite readers of The Elements of Social Scientific Thinking to share their assessments with us. We can be reached at the Department of Political Science, Western Washington University, Bellingham, WA 98225, or we can be contacted by e-mail at *Ken.Hoover@wwu.edu* or *donovan@cc.wwu.edu*.

Acknowledgments

A work that endures for more than a quarter of a century has, in a real sense, many authors—too many to list. We have relied upon the comments of, first of all, our students, to whom we are most grateful.

Numerous critics and colleagues have made valuable suggestions. Bob Blair of the College of Wooster in Ohio helped greatly in shaping the first edition. Over several editions, the comments of

Aage Clausen, Emeritus Professor of Political Science at the Ohio State University, were crucial in maintaining the distinctive mission and tone of the book. More recently, several colleagues have provided particular insights: Shaun Bowler of the University of California—Riverside, and, at Western Washington University, Carl Simpson, Dana Jack, Sara Weir, and John Richardson. To all of these, full pardon and many thanks.

We would also like to thank the reviewers who contributed their ideas and opinions on the revision of this text: Shelia Cordray of Oregon State University, Jeffrey A. Halley and Richard J. Harris of the University of Texas at San Antonio, and James Riddlesperger of Texas Christian University.

Judy Hoover contributed ideas to the writing and a great deal more; and Andrew and Erin Hoover have survived the embarrassment of being used as an example in one chapter to become professional users of words in their own right.

László Moholy-Nagy's art has distinguished the covers of all eight editions. His A II (1922), framed in various colors, graced the first five editions. With the addition of Todd Donovan as co-author of the sixth edition, the cover image was changed to AL 3 (1925). For the seventh edition, the image is of Moholy-Nagy's most advanced work in the series, A 18 (1927). For this edition, the painting is A XIII (1926). It may be viewed at the Norton Simon Museum in Pasadena, Calfornia.

A Bauhaus modernist and aesthetic radical, Moholy-Nagy mingled the utopian impulses of post–World War I art with reflections of the utilitarian turn emanating from the Russian Revolution. Moholy-Nagy was, however, too idiosyncratic ever to be confined by a political program, and he let his aesthetic vision take him beyond orthodoxies—old and new.

Moholy-Nagy practiced art as a "way of life," aimed toward the "development of collective individuality," according to Krisztina Passuth, in her book *Moholy-Nagy* (Thames and Hudson, 1985, p. 14). This message fits with the purpose of our book, which is to equip each reader to seek greater insight into society and, at the same time, to share those insights with others in ways that will improve the human condition.

The initial choice of Moholy-Nagy's work came from a visit to the Guggenheim Museum by book designer Margaret Dodd. Subsequent editors have maintained the tradition and, with this edition for Wadsworth Publishing, we wish to thank David Tatom and his colleagues for keeping up the good work.

About the Authors

Kenneth Hoover (Ph.D., University of Wisconsin—Madison) is Professor of Political Science at Western Washington University. Recent books include *Economics as Ideology: Keynes, Laski Hayek and the Creation of Contemporary Politics* (Rowman Littlefield, Lanham, MD: 2003) and Kenneth Hoover with John Miles, Vernon Johnson, and Sara Weir, *Ideology and Political Life*, 3rd ed. (Wadsworth, 2001).

Todd Donovan (Ph.D., University of California—Riverside) is Professor of Political Science at Western Washington University. Recent books include Todd Donovan and Shaun Bowler, *Reforming the Republic: Electoral Institutions for the New America* (2004) and Shaun Bowler, Todd Donovan, and David Brockington, *Electoral Reform and Minority Representation: Local Experiments with Alternative Elections* (2003).

The Elements
of Social Scientific
Thinking

PREVIEW OF CHAPTER ONE

THINKING SCIENTIFICALLY

"Science searches the common experience of people; and it is made by people, and it has their style."

–JACOB BRONOWSKI

"Social science" in cold print gives rise to images of some robot in a statistics laboratory reducing human activity to bloodless digits and simplified formulas. Research reports filled with mechanical-sounding words such as "empirical," "quantitative," "operational," "inverse," and "correlative" aren't very poetic. Yet the stereotypes of social science created by these images are, we will try to show, wrong.

Like any other mode of knowing, social science can be used for perverse ends; however, it can also be used for humane personal understanding. By testing thoughts against observations of reality, science helps liberate inquiry from bias, prejudice, and just plain muddle-headedness. So it is unwise to be put off by simple stereotypes—too many people accept these stereotypes and deny themselves the power of social scientific understanding.

The word **science** stands for a very great deal in our culture—some even consider it the successor to religion in the modern age. Our objective here is not to examine the whole tangle of issues associated with science; it is to find a path into the scientific way of thinking about things. In order to find that path, we will begin by allowing some descriptions of science to emerge out of contrasts with other forms of knowledge.

First, we have to identify some distractions that should be ignored. Science is sometimes confused with **technology**, which is the application of science to various tasks. Grade-school texts that caption pictures of voyages to the planets with the title "Science Marches On!" aid such confusion. The technology that makes such voyages possible emerged from the use of scientific strategies in the study of propulsion, electronics, and numerous other fields. It is the mode of inquiry that is scientific; the spacecraft is a piece of technology.

Just as science is not technology, neither is it some specific body of knowledge. The popular phrase, "Science tells us [for example] that smoking can kill you," really misleads. "Science" doesn't tell us anything; people tell us things—in this case, people who have used scientific strategies to investigate the relationship of smoking to cancer. Science, as a way of thought and investigation, is best conceived of as existing not in books, or in machinery, or in reports containing numbers, but rather in that invisible world of the mind. Science has to do with the way questions are formulated and answered; it is a set of rules and forms for inquiry created by people who want reliable answers.

Another distraction comes from identifying particular people as "scientists." That usage isn't false, since the people so labeled practice the scientific form of inquiry; but neither is it fully honest to say that some people are scientists, whereas others are nonscientists. Some people specialize in scientific approaches to knowledge, but we are all participants in the scientific way of thinking. Science is a mode of inquiry that is · common to all human beings.

In becoming more self-conscious of your own habits of thought, you will find that there is a bit of the scientist in all of us. We measure, compare, modify beliefs, and acquire a kind of savvy about evidence in the daily business of figuring out what to do next and how to relate to others. The simplest of games involves the testing of tactics and strategies against the data of performance, and that is crudely scientific. Even trying out different styles of dress for their impact on others has an element of science in it.

The scientific way of thought is one of a number of strategies by which we try to cope with a vital reality: the uncertainty of life. We don't know what the consequences of many of our actions will be. We may have little idea of the forces that affect us subtly or directly, gradually or suddenly. In trying to accomplish even the simplest task, such as figuring out what to eat, we do elementary calculations of what might taste good or what might be good for us. If there's enough uncertainty on that score, a little advance testing is a good idea: the queen has her taster, and the rest of us—at least when it comes to a certain hamburger— have the assurance that billions have already been sold.

· Science is a process of thinking and asking questions, not a body of knowledge. It is one of several ways of claiming that we know something. In one sense, the scientific method is a set of criteria for deciding how conflicts about differing views of reality can be resolved. It offers a strategy that researchers can use when approaching a question. It offers consumers of research the ability to critically assess how evidence has been developed and used in reaching a conclusion.

The scientific approach has many competitors in the search for understanding. For many people throughout most of history, the competitors have prevailed. Analysis of reality has usually been much less popular than myths, superstitions, and hunches, which have the reassuring feel of certainty *before* the event they try to predict or control, though seldom afterward. Sometimes unverified belief sponsors an inspired action or sustains the doubtful until a better day. Certainly personal beliefs are a vital part of our lives. The point is that the refusal to analyze is crippling, and the skilled analyst is in a position of strength.

Why Bother to Be Systematic?

Most human communication takes place among small groups of people who share a common language and much common experience and understanding of the world they live in. There is a ready-made arena for mutual agreement. Not so in a more complex social environment. Although families can transmit wisdom across generations by handing down stories and maxims, societies run into trouble. In its most cynical form, the question is, "Whose story is to be believed?" The need to understand what is happening around us and to share experiences with others makes systematic thought and inquiry essential.

Because society is interesting for the drama it contains, there is a tendency to dispense with systematic understanding and get on with the descriptions, stories, and personal judgments. Although these can be illuminating, they often have limited usefulness because highly subjective accounts of life form a poor basis for the development of common understanding and common action.

* The intricate task of getting people to bridge the differences that arise from the singularity of their experience requires a disciplined approach to knowledge. Knowledge is socially powerful only if it is knowledge that can be put to use. Social knowledge, if it is to be useful, must be communicable, valid, and compelling.

In order to be **communicable**, knowledge must be expressed in clear form. And if the knowledge is intended to be used as a spur to action, it must be valid in light of the appropriate evidence and **compelling** in the way that it fits the question raised. A personal opinion such as, "I think that capitalism exploits the poor," may influence your friends and even your relatives to think that there is some injustice in our society. But it probably won't make any waves with others. If, however, you can cite evidence that more than one in six American children live in poverty, a more compelling argument results, because you relate a judgment to a measurement of reality.[1] People who don't even like you but who favor some kind of fairness in wealth distribution might find such a statement a powerful cue to examine our economic system critically. Knowledge built on evidence, and captured in clear transmissible form, makes for power over the environment.

Accumulating knowledge so that past mistakes can be avoided has always intrigued civilized humanity. One can record the sayings of wise people, and that does contribute greatly to cultural enrichment. Yet there is surely room for another kind of cumulative effort: the building up of statements evidenced in a manner that can be double-checked by others. To double-check a statement requires that one know precisely what was claimed and how the claim was tested. This is a major part of the enterprise of science. The steps to be discussed in Chapter Two in the section on the scientific method are the guideposts for accomplishing that kind of knowing.

The Role of Reasoned Judgment and Opinion

All this vaguely ominous talk about systematic thinking is not meant to cast out reasoned judgment, opinion, and imagination. After all, there is no particular sense in limiting the facilities of the mind in any inquiry.

---

[1]See National Center for Children in Poverty, "Low Income Children in the United States: A Brief Demographic Profile." Mailman School of Public Health. Columbia University. April 4, 2002 (*http://www.nccp.org*). This report used U.S. Census Bureau data from March 1976 to March 2001, and notes that 15.8 percent of children lived in poverty. This was the lowest level of child poverty since 1978.

Reasoned judgment is a staple of human understanding. A reasoned judgment bears a respectable relationship to evidence. Because people inevitably have to act in the absence of complete evidence for decision making, the term "judgment" is important. Judgment connotes decision making in which all the powers of the mind are activated to make the best use of available knowledge.

Social science does not eliminate the role of judgment from the research process. Indeed, judgment plays a crucial role in how scientific evidence is gathered and evaluated. We can observe that the top 10 percent of U.S. households have fifty-five times more income than the poorest 10 percent. The income of the richest grew by 15 percent during the most recent economic boom, while income of the poor remained stagnant. It is another matter, however, to link this evidence to broad social questions about capitalism, inequality, poverty, wealth, exploitation, productivity, economic development, and other issues. Logic and good judgment are required to interpret the evidence.[2]

Reasoned judgment is the first part of systematic thought. The proposition that "A full moon on the eve of election day promotes liberal voting" could be correct, but it does not reflect much reasoned judgment, since there is neither evidence for linking the two events nor a logical connection between them. An investigator with time and resources might look into such a proposition, but in a world of scarce time, inadequate resources, and serious problems of social analysis to engage rare talents, such an investigation makes little sense.[3] Although the proposition may be intuitive, even intuition usually bears some relationship to experience and evidence.

---

[2]Shannon McCaffery, "Income Gap Growing." Associated Press Wire Service (January 18, 2000). Richard W. Stevenson, "Income Gap Widens Between Rich and Poor in 5 States and Narrows in 1." *New York Times* (April 24, 2002). Michael Hout and Samuel Lucas, "Narrowing the Income Gap between Rich and Poor," *Chronicle of Higher Education,* Section 2 (August 16, 1996), B1–B2. These studies show that in 1996 the income gap between rich and poor was the largest since 1921, and was growing.

[3]However, police and bartenders will tell you that the night of a full moon does, in fact, bring out some pretty bizarre behavior; the hypothesis isn't completely preposterous.

Opinion, likewise, plays an inescapable role in scientific analysis, because all efforts at inquiry proceed from some personal interest or other. No one asks a question unless there is an interest in what the conclusion might be. Furthermore, each person's angle of vision on reality is necessarily slightly different from the angle of another. Opinion can't be eliminated from inquiry, but it can be controlled so that it does not fly off into complete fantasy. One practice that assists in reducing the role of opinion is for the researcher to be conscious of his or her values and opinions.

Plato's famous aphorism, "Know thyself," applies here. Much damage has been done to the cause of good social science by those who pretend **objectivity** to the point at which their research conceals opinions that covertly structure their conclusions. No one is truly objective, certainly not about the nature of society—there are too many personal stakes involved for that.

Ultimately, good science provides its own check on the influence of values in an inquiry. If the method by which the study has been done and the evidence for conclusions are clearly and fully stated, the study can be examined for the fit of conclusions to evidence. If there is doubt about the validity of what has been done, the study itself can be double-checked, or "replicated," to use the technical term. This feature distinguishes science from personal judgment and protects against personal bias.

No one can double-check everything that goes on, as the mind deals with inner feelings, perceptions of experience, and thought processes. Science brings the steps of inquiry out of the mind and into public view so that they can be shared as part of the process of accumulating knowledge.

The Role of Imagination, Intuition, and Custom

The mind, in its many ways of knowing, is never so clever or so mysterious as in the exercise of **imagination.** If there is any sense in which people can leap over tall obstacles in a single bound, it is in the flight of the mind. But it is one thing to imagine a possible proposition about reality, and it is quite another to start imagining evidence.

Science is really a matter of figuring out relationships between things we know something about. To propose a relationship is a creative and imaginative act; however, much systematic preparation may lie in the background. To test a proposition against reality involves a different order of imagination—mainly, the ability to find in the bits and pieces of information elicited from reality the one item that is essential to testing the credibility of a particular idea.

It is in the realm of discovery that science becomes a direct partner of imagination. The history of natural science is filled with examples, from the realization that the earth revolves around the sun, and not vice versa, to the discovery that matter is made up of tiny atoms. Each of these discoveries was made by bold and imaginative people who were not afraid to challenge a whole structure of customary belief by consulting evidence in the real world. Although these were discoveries on a grand scale, the same sort of effort is involved in stepping outside accepted explanations of human behavior to imagine other possibilities and test them by the intelligent use of evidence. Feminists do this when they examine traditional claims about male–female differences. To be truly imaginative is something like trying to escape gravity— the initial move is the hardest. Even though the social sciences have as yet few discoveries to compare with the feats of natural science, the application of science to social relations is a much more recent and vastly more complicated undertaking.[4]

---

[4]Perhaps one of the earliest attempts to confront social custom with science was the effort in the late 19th century by Francis Galton, an English scientist, to test the efficacy of prayer. Observing that prayers were daily offered in churches throughout the land for the long life of royalty, he compared their longevity to that of the gentry and a variety of professionals. He found, after excluding deaths by accident or violence, and including only those who survived their thirtieth year, that the average age of decease for royalty was 64.04 years, the lowest for all his categories. Galton did observe, however, that prayer has many personal uses aside from the fulfillment of requests. And, who knows, royalty might have died sooner but for such petitions. P. B. Medwar, *Induction and Intuition in Scientific Thought* (Philadelphia: American Philosophical Society, 1969), pp. 2–7.

At a fundamental level, scientific inquiry is motivated by curiosity and a desire to find order in what may seem to be chaos. We see an array of confusing events, incidents, and behavior and have an urge to know why something happened or what event caused another. Social science allows us to satisfy our curiosity and to gain understanding for its own sake. On another level, social science produces knowledge that is communicable and can be used to explain our understanding to others.

Whatever we may come to say about the careful thinking that scientific analysis requires, there is still no way to capture completely the wondrous process of "having an idea." Science is absolutely not a system for frustrating that exercise of intuition and imagination; rather, it is a set of procedures for making such ideas as fruitful and productive as human ingenuity allows. Even the most wonderful idea is only as good as its relationship to some present or potential reality. Science is the art of reality testing, of taking ideas and confronting them with observable evidence drawn from the phenomena to which they relate.

To step back from the general blur of human relationships and envision alternative possibilities demands a level of imagination that is as uncommon as it is necessary. In the usual run of social and political experience, David Hume's observation may be sadly accurate: "[People], once accustomed to obedience, never think of departing from that path in which they and their ancestors trod and to which they are confined by so many urgent and visible motives."[5] Yet it is in the understanding and reform of social and political arrangements that the world requires the very best application of disciplined imagination. In the absence of imaginative efforts to understand the reality of society, we are confined to the beaten path of custom and the inequities that stifle human potential.

We also may be confined to some very unproductive habits of behavior. It used to be the custom in England to hang

[5]David Hume, "Of the Origins of Government," *Political Essays,* ed. Charles Hendel (New York: Liberal Arts Press, 1953), p. 41.

pickpockets publicly in order to discourage others in the trade. Someone noticed, however, that more pockets were picked at pickpocket hangings than at other public events. The custom survived that bit of social science far longer than it should have.

Custom is not all bad, for it may embody the lessons learned from a long, often unhappy, experience with reality—and it is, in a vague way, scientific. Custom frequently holds communities together in the face of enormous and even violent pressures. Yet the task of any social science must be to understand why things are the way they are, as well as how the elements of social life can be reformed to allow for more humane patterns of personal development and expression. The weapons in this struggle for understanding are not only science with its procedures for disciplining inquiry but also the intuition that life can be better than it is, that a given pattern of behavior may be other than inevitable, that even the smallest transactions of behavior may contain the keys to larger structures of possibility and potential.

The method of any effort at understanding involves a tension between thought and investigation. There are various ways of linking these two components. The mystic perceives an inner truth and interprets "signs" as validation of the insight. The historian looks for patterns in the past and then suggests their usefulness in interpreting the meanings of events. Thus, the "rise of the middle class" in Europe becomes a major interpretive concept for the historian. Someone who is scientific attempts to be more concrete than the mystic and more precise than the historian with respect to the thoughts by which research is guided, the data regarded as significant in the investigation, and the measures used in testing mental constructions against reality.

In the chapters that follow, we will look at the steps involved in building scientific understanding one at a time. As you will see, the technique requires common sense more than technical knowledge or elaborate preparation.

• Concepts Introduced

Science	Opinion
Technology	Objectivity
Communicable knowledge	Imagination
Valid knowledge	Intuition
Compelling knowledge	Custom
Reasoned judgment	

• Questions for Discussion

1. What are examples of nonscientific modes of understanding? How might these nonscientific modes be used to explain the following?

- Why some nations are wealthier than others
- Why political revolutions occur in some places but not in others
- Who will win next year's World Series

2. How is social scientific knowledge more powerful than other forms of knowledge (e.g., intuition, custom)? What are its shortcomings and dangers?

3. How might scientific knowledge be useful to someone who is concerned with reforming or changing society?

4. Why is imagination essential to social science?

5. Is the application of imagination more important to social science than to natural science (e.g., chemistry, biology)?

PREVIEW OF CHAPTER TWO

- The Origin and Utility of Concepts
- What Is a Variable?
  - Quantification and Measurement:
  - Turning Concepts into Variables
  - Reliability and Validity of Variables
- The Hypothesis
- The Scientific Method
- The Many Roles of Theory

Chapter Two

THE ELEMENTS OF SCIENCE

"[Scientific inquiry]

begins as a story about a

Possible World—a story

which we invent and

criticize and modify as

we go along, so that it

ends by being, as nearly

as we can make it, a story

about real life."

—P. B. MEDAWAR

To see scientific thought in the context of other kinds of thinking, as we have tried to do, tells us why we should be interested in science. Now it is time to see what science is made of.

The elements of a scientific strategy are, in themselves, simple to understand. They are concepts, variables, hypotheses, measurements, and theories. The way in which these are combined constitutes the scientific method. It is the function of theory to give meaning and motivation to this method by enabling us to interpret what is observed. First, we will try to put each element in place.

The Origin and Utility of Concepts

If you had to purge all words and other symbols from your mind and confront the world with a virgin mind, what would you do? Without a body to sustain, you might do nothing. The necessities of survival, however, start closing in, and the first act of the mind might be to sort out the edible objects from the inedible, then the warm from the cold, the friendly from the hostile. From there it isn't very far to forming concepts like food, shelter, and warmth, and symbolizing these concepts in the form of words or utterances. Thus, humbly, emerges the instrument called language. The search for truly usable concepts and categories is under way. Languages are nothing more than huge collections of **concepts**—names for things, feelings, and ideas generated or acquired by people in the course of relating to each other and to their environment.

Some concepts and classifications might not be very helpful. To conceptualize all plants under only a single designation would preclude further distinctions between those that are edible, those that heal, and those that poison. Some concepts relate to experience too vaguely: English has but one word for something so various and complicated as love. Greek allows three concepts: *eros* for romantic love, *agape* for generalized feelings of affection and *filios* for family love. The inadequacy of English in dealing with the concept of love affects everyone's experience through the tricky ways the word is used in our culture.

Notice that reality testing is built right into the process of naming things, one of the most elementary transactions of existence. That back-and-forth between the stimuli of the environment and the reflections of the mind makes up the kind of thought we will be trying to capture for analysis.

After several thousand years of history, we still have to face the fact that the process of naming things is difficult. Language emerges essentially by agreement. You and I and the other members of the family (tribe, state, nation, world) agree, for example, to call things that twinkle in the sky stars. Unfortunately, these agreements may not be very precise. In common usage, the term "star" covers a multitude of objects, big and small, hot and cold, solid and gaseous.

To call a thing by a precise name is the beginning of understanding, because it is the key to the procedure that allows the mind to grasp reality and its many relationships. It makes a great deal of difference whether an illness is conceived of as caused by an evil spirit or by bacteria on a binge. The concept *bacteria* is tied to a system of concepts in which there is a connection to a powerful repertory of treatments, that is, antibiotics.

To capture meaning in language is a profound and subtle process, even if it is a little sloppy. For example, the abstract concept race expresses differences in the way that groups are identified. When names are given to categories or properties of race, the problems, power, and difficulty of naming things become evident. Researchers often name people "white" or "nonwhite" (or "Anglo" or "non-Anglo") when using simplistic classifications of race. Such a distinction, although common practice, trivializes differences among a large portion of the world's people. Also, the names themselves can raise complex issues. Think of the various names used in the United States to refer to African Americans (Negro, African American, person of color, black) or Hispanic Americans (Latino, Latina, Hispanic, person of color, Latin American, Mexican American, Central American, Puerto Rican, etc.).

Naming is a process that can give the namer great power. Properties of the concept *race* are not easily named. Names of races, moreover, confer different identities on different people. In your own expression of social scientific thinking, although you are invited to be precise about concepts, you are not invited to be arrogant about the utility of your new knowledge for reworking lives, societies, and civilizations.

The importance of having the right name for a thing can hardly be overestimated. Thomas Hobbes, a seventeenth-century political theorist, thought the proper naming of things so important to the establishment of political order that he made it a central function of the sovereign. King James understood the message and ordered an authoritative translation of the Bible as a way of overcoming violent squabbles about the precise meanings of words in the Scriptures.

More germane to the modern scene, George Orwell, in his antiutopian novel *1984*, gave us a vision of a whole bureaucracy devoted to reconstructing language concepts to enhance the power of a totalitarian society. In recent U.S. political history, President Clinton attempted to defuse controversy about his relations with Monica Lewinsky by redefining the concept of sexual relations between consenting adults. These examples are intended to make you aware that by tinkering with the meanings of concepts, one can play with the foundations of human understanding and social control.

But it will be a while before you master the scientific method sufficiently to pull off anything very grand. For now, the point is that, for scientific purposes, concepts are (1) tentative, (2) based on agreement, and (3) useful only to the degree that they capture or isolate some significant and definable item in reality.

What have concepts got to do with science? If you've spent any time around babies, you might notice that they often try to show off by pointing at things and naming them. It gets a little boring the tenth or fifteenth time through, but babies take justifiable pride in the exercise. Next come sentences. From naming things, from being able to symbolize something rather than simply pointing at it, comes the next step in moving reality around so it can produce things that are needed. The first sentence Andrew Hoover spoke was to his sister Erin. Sitting on a little cart, he said, "Erin, push me!" She did.

What you are reading now is an effort to link concepts in order to expand your understanding. People speak sentences by the thousands in an attempt to move reality to some useful response. Most people don't have the good luck Andrew did on his first try. Often the concepts are confusing and the connections are vague or unlikely, not to mention the problem that the speaker has with the listener's perceptions and motives.

Thought and theory develop through the linking of concepts. Consider, as an example, Pierre Proudhon's famous proposition, "Property is theft!" Property, as a concept, stands for the notion that a person can claim sole ownership of land or other resources. Theft, of course, means the act of taking something without justification. By linking these two concepts through the verb "is," Proudhon meant to equate the institution of private property with the denial of humankind's common ownership of nature's resources. The concept of privately owned property was, he thought, unjustifiable thievery. While Proudhon's declaration illustrates the linkage of concepts at the lofty philosophical level, the humblest sentence performs the same operation.

Science is a way of checking on the formulation of concepts and testing the possible linkages between them through references to observable phenomena. The next step is to see how scientists turn concepts into something that can be observed. When concepts are defined as variables, they can be used to form a special kind of sentence, the hypothesis.

What Is a Variable?

A **variable** is a name for something that is thought to influence (or be influenced by) a particular state of being in something else. Heat is one variable in making water boil, and so is pressure. Age has been established as a modestly important variable in voting; however, there are many other more significant variables: socioeconomic standing, parental influence, race, gender, region of residence, and so on.

A variable is, in addition, a special kind of concept that contains within it a notion of degree or differentiation. Temperature is an easily understood example of a variable. It includes the notion of more or less heat—that is, of degree. As the name suggests, variables are things that vary. Interesting questions in social science center on concepts that involve variation and how changes in one phenomenon help to explain variation in another.

Consider, as an example, the relationship between religion and voting. In the first place, religion is a different kind of variable than, say, temperature. Although there may be such a thing as degrees of "religiosity,"[1] it is likely we would discuss variation in the concept *religion* in terms of religious denominations. There is substantial variation in the religions with which people identify. For example, exit poll data were used to assess the importance of religion in the 2000 election when Democratic presidential candidate Al Gore won the popular vote with 48.4 percent support, over 47.9 percent for Republican George W. Bush and 2.7 percent for Green candidate Ralph Nader. Bush won the Electoral College vote and thus the presidency after the Supreme Court halted a controversial recount in Florida. Data collected by the *Los Angeles Times* found that fully 80 percent of Jewish voters supported Gore (compared to 17 percent for Bush and 1 percent for Nader), whereas 63 percent of Protestants voted for Bush (compared to 34 percent for Gore and 2 percent for Nader). Fifty-two percent of Catholics voted for Bush, while 45 percent voted for Gore. Gore won majorities among those with "other" religions, and among those claiming no religious affiliation.[2] Data such as these permit us to say something meaningful about the relationship between the variable *religion* and the variable *voting behavior.*

Although most variables deal with differences of degree, as in temperature, or differences of variety, as in religion, some variables are even simpler. These deal with the most elementary kind of variation: present or absent, there or not there, existent or nonexistent. Take pregnancy, for example. There is no such thing as a little bit of it. Either the condition exists or it doesn't.

Turning concepts into variables, dull as it may seem, is a very creative process and often raises intriguing questions. Consider,

---

[1]Various attempts have been made to measure degree of individual "religiosity" in terms of attitudinal and behavioral traits such as regularity of church attendance. For an example, see Lyman A. Kellstedt and Mark A. Noll, "Religion, Voting for President and Party Identification, 1948–1984," *Religion and American Politics: From the Colonial Period to the 1980s,* ed. Mark A. Noll (Oxford, England: Oxford University Press, 1990), p. 347.

[2]CNN.com Election 2000 Report. "Exit Polls." At *http://www.cnn.com/ ELECTION/2000/results/index.epolls.html,* accessed Dec 2, 2002.

as an illustration, such an ordinary variable as time. The early Greeks puzzled a good deal over how to conceptualize this variable. It seems obvious that time has to be thought of as having a beginning—so philosophers went about trying to figure out when the beginning was. Yet the nagging question always popped up: What happened before that?

Plato and Aristotle both played with the idea that time might not be linear at all; that is, it might not have a beginning, a progression, and presumably an end. It just might be cyclical! This seems crazy to us children of linear time, but they were thinking that universal time might be something like the cycle of the body, a rhythm found everywhere in nature. Historic time, therefore, might best be conceived of as an unfolding structure of events in which one follows the other until the whole pattern is played out and the entire cycle starts over again. Aristotle commented that it just might be that he himself "was living before the Fall of Troy quite as much as after it, since, when the wheel of fortune had turned through another cycle, the Trojan War would be re-enacted and Troy would fall again."[3]

The social science done by introductory students seldom involves such mind-boggling conceptual problems, yet it wouldn't do to pretend that these problems don't exist. The variable *personality,* for example, is reputed to have more than four hundred definitions in the professional literature, partly because personality is a compound of a huge range of other variables: class, status, self-concept, race, socialization, and so forth. The complexity of personality as a variable has driven social scientists to such awkward definitions as "One's acquired, relatively enduring, yet dynamic, unique system of predispositions to psychological and social behavior."[4]

[3]Stephen Toulmin and June Goodfield, *The Discovery of Time* (New York: Harper and Row, 1965), p. 46.
[4]Gordon DiRenzo, *Personality and Politics* (Garden City, N.Y.: Anchor Books, 1974), p. 16.

Even when social scientists agree on the description of a variable, that doesn't mean the definition possesses the qualities of eternal truth—it just means that some people who have thought about it carefully agree that a given definition seems to help answer some questions. Moreover, researchers often settle on a definition of a variable for reasons of convenience. Party identification in the United States is conventionally measured by survey question responses that place voters on a continuum reflecting their identification with the two major political parties. The continuum is represented by this seven-point scale:

←strong Dem—weak Dem—Ind leaning
Dem—Ind—Ind leaning Rep—weak Rep—strong Rep→

Political independents are assumed to be in the center of the political spectrum. Yet the truth of the matter might be that many "independents" think of themselves as radicals who are outside the center. Some might be so nonpartisan or apolitical that they just don't think of themselves in terms of political parties at all. Furthermore, some "leaning" independents are nearly as partisan in their voting as "weak" partisans.[5] Although this definition of the variable might not perfectly reflect the underlying truth of the concept *partisanship*, it continues to have predictive power. The question has been asked on surveys for decades, so it allows researchers to evaluate trends in partisanship over time. As the difficulties of categorizing independents on this spectrum become apparent, new definitions of partisanship will emerge. Ignoring the problem of specifying how concepts should be turned into variables doesn't make the problem go away, it just gets you further into the linguistic soup.

The huge stock of concepts in language creates enormous possibilities for linking up variables to explain events. People have muddled around for centuries trying to sort through signifi-

---

[5]William Flanigan and Nancy Zingale, *Political Behavior of the American Electorate,* 10th ed. (Washington, D.C.: Congressional Quarterly Press, 2002), pp. 85–87. These authors note that the American electorate is becoming "more nonpartisan overall, but not invariably more independent" as more nonpartisans fail even to call themselves independent.

cant connections. Science is a slightly elevated form of muddling by which these connections are tried out and tested as carefully as possible. In medical science, it took centuries to isolate the many variables affecting disease. Only recently has medical science become so disciplined that it can diagnose many diseases through highly significant blood-chemistry analysis. This development represents the present stage of a long process of isolating and eliminating a host of unimportant or marginally significant variables. Increasingly, Western doctors come up against an ancient form of medicine developed to a high art in China, and now we have medical scientists trying to figure out why acupuncture works. Whole new sets of variables must be considered, new conceptual bridges built, and the resistance of conventional understanding overcome.

Unfortunately for social science, we have barely figured out how to lay the foundation for a structure of theory to explain social behavior. Many new students of social science do not see—especially when confronted by thick texts in introductory courses—the context of struggle and accomplishment, tentativeness and probability, behind what has been achieved in social understanding.

Social science currently contains many subdivisions (e.g., political science, sociology, economics, psychology, education), all of which are working on defining, observing, and linking specific variables within subsystems of behavior. Social scientists are in the process of chasing a good many possible connections between variables. The bits of tested knowledge that do emerge await an integration across the lines of these inquiries. Relatively few have been attempted, though these efforts are bound to increase in view of the dramatic need for comprehensive social understanding.

Quantification and Measurement: Turning Concepts into Variables

We said earlier that social scientists turn concepts into variables. This is done so the concept can be expressed in a form that is observable and includes some notion of degree or differentiation.

The next question is: How does one pin down that degree or differentiation? The answer involves a two-step process: quantification and measurement.

The idea of quantification means setting up a standard amount of a thing and putting a label on it. When we do this, we make it possible to express abstract concepts (such as length) in a manner that provides a common reference for observation. The origins of some quantifications are pretty strange. The ancient Greeks, for example, needed a standard quantity of distance, so they settled on the length of Hercules' foot. For a long time the foot competed with the cubit, which was the length of someone else's forearm. The trouble with the cubit was that people could never agree on how long the standard forearm was—some said 17 inches, some said 21 inches. Consequently, we don't hear much about cubits anymore.

Isolating standardized units increases the power of description and analysis. When Gabriel Fahrenheit established the idea of a degree of temperature, he made possible a much more useful description of hot and cold. It makes a considerable difference with respect to a puddle of water if the temperature is 32 degrees rather than 33 degrees; the words "cold" and "colder" don't work very well for capturing that vital degree of difference.

Quantification in social science takes two forms: discrete and continuous. **Discrete quantification** relates to counting the presence or absence of a thing. It also relates to counting differences of quality as they are captured in categories. A vote for a candidate is a discrete and specific act that can be counted in a conventional manner. A person's sex is a quality that can be counted as being either male or female.

Some quantifications, however, have to capture the notion of variation along a continuum. Age is an example of a **continuous quantification.** True, one can count the number of years in a person's age, but the quantification of age is an expression of something that is ongoing. One of the authors of this book is 62.29 years old today; next September he will be 63 years old. Continuous quantification deals not with discrete items but with dimensions like age, length, and time. The mark of continuous quantification is that the variable involved may have any value on a scale, whereas in discrete quantification, only whole numbers appear (as in counting sheep).

Each variable has its own peculiar problems and potentials for quantification. One of the distinguishing characteristics of a well-developed science is the array of quantifiable variables that are useful to people working in the field. One of the marks of a smart scientist is the ability to find ways of quantifying important variables in a reliable and meaningful way. Economics has come a long way by using money as a unit of analysis (though economists, among others, sometimes confuse money with value). Many powerful economic indicators, such as the gross domestic product or the consumer price index, are based on money.

Unfortunately for the other social sciences, there aren't such easily quantifiable units for measuring power or representing psychological stress, alienation, happiness, personal security, or, for that matter, value. Yet inventive scientists have found more or less successful ways of capturing quantifiable pieces of these variables. A text in any of these areas contains dozens of illustrations of how concepts are turned into quantifiable variables, and we will see some of them in the next chapter. The importance of quantification is that when it can be accomplished, there is potential for more precise measurement.

Measurement is not something we choose to do or not do—it is inherent in every analytic discussion. If you doubt this, listen carefully in the next conversation you have and notice your dependence on terms that imply measurement. A simple political statement such as, "Democrats generally favor the poor," involves three bits of measurement. The verb "favor" implies degrees of difference; so does the term "poor"; and "Democrats" is a classification. The modifier "generally" attempts to qualify the measurement by indicating that it is not a universal characteristic of all Democrats.

If quantities can be established, measurement becomes much easier. The most obvious measurement deals with the problem of how much: how much distance, how much money, and so forth. Some questions of how much are not so easy to measure—public opinion, for example. Using responses to questions as the quantifiable unit of analysis, one crude survey technique provides respondents a "forced choice" and divides opinion into favorable versus unfavorable. Here, opinion is quantified as a discrete, categorical variable: "Are you for it or against it?" Public-opinion polling is often done on this basis. One thing such a simple measurement conceals, of course, is the intensity of the opinion. On many political issues there may be minorities that are passionately on one side and majorities that are lukewarmly on the other side. Some public-opinion polls deal with this by using four categories instead of two:

Strongly For   For   Against   Strongly Against

A political system that simply acts on majority sentiment without taking intensity into account can get itself into a lot of trouble—as this nation did over the Vietnam War. A passionate minority of opponents became embittered and alienated by the reliance of policy makers on a rather unenthusiastic majority of supporters. It took several years for the minority to become a majority able to change policy.

A fancier way of measuring intensity of preferences is to measure opinion in terms of degree. Some surveys ask people to evaluate candidates or parties on a "feeling thermometer" scale where 0 is negative, 50 is neutral, and 100 is positive. This helps expand the range of responses and reveals more accurately the state of opinion, but it may still conceal a great deal of information. It seems that some people may give responses to questions even if they don't really have much of an opinion on the matter.[6]

---

[6]Problems with nonattitudes are discussed in Herbert Asher, *Polling and the Public: What Every Citizen Should Know*, 4th ed. (Washington, DC: Congressional Quarterly Press, 1998), chapter 2.

TABLE 2.1 MEASURING FEELINGS ABOUT PRESIDENTIAL AND VICE-
PRESIDENTIAL CANDIDATES, 2000

	Average Rating	% of People Rating at "50"	% of People Unable to Rank
Al Gore, Jr	57	15%	2 %
George W. Bush	56	18	3
John McCain	60	25	21
Dick Cheney	56	28	24
Ralph Nader	52	30	27
Joseph Lieberman	57	28	27
Pat Buchanan	39	31	18
Bill Bradley	55	34	28

SOURCE: Authors' calculations from raw data files—2000 American National Election Study. Raw data available at: *http://www.umich.edu/~nes/*.

Consider response to "feeling thermometer" questions about candidates running for president in 2000. As Table 2.1 illustrates, the proportion of people who had neutral feelings about the candidate seems related to the proportion who had actually heard of the candidate. Relatively unknown candidates (Pat Buchanan and Ralph Nader) received far more scores of "50" than well-known candidates like George W. Bush and Al Gore. This leads some to wonder whether this question is a valid measure of neutral "feelings" about lesser known candidates, or whether it measures "nonattitudes" or something else.

Reliability and Validity of Variables

Quantified measurement of variables, properly conceived and executed, has the potential for specifying differentiation and degree more effectively than fuzzy words in vague sentences. However we decide to measure variables, we hope to find a method of counting that would provide reliable results if it were used by other researchers.

As an example, we could decide to measure "presidential approval" by asking a random sample of respondents if they "like" or "dislike" the president, thereby forcing a choice between only two alternatives. We might expect that other researchers could use the same measure the next day with a comparable random sample and produce results similar to ours. Conversely, we might ask the first four people we see on a bus to "discuss what they think" about the president. We could then rate presidential approval based on our personal impression of their responses. Other researchers using this measure the next day on the same bus might produce wildly different results. The answers might be vague, and the values influencing the interpretation may differ.

Measurement of a variable is said to be reliable if it produces the same result when different people use it. The forced-choice question would probably produce consistent results, because each researcher using comparable samples simply has to count up the number of "likes" and "dislikes" to find a measure of approval. Open-ended discussions with people on the bus, however, require that the researcher interpret a variety of comments that might (or might not) reflect approval. The answers are meaningful—in some ways even more meaningful than the forced-choice responses. But they are less likely to get us a reliable answer to the question of presidential popularity.

Theoretical concerns about measures of variables can be subtle. Each measure we use is supposed to do a good job of representing the underlying truth of the abstract concept we claim to be representing with a quantified variable. A measure is said to be *valid* "if it does what it is intended to do."[7] The closer a quantified measure comes to reflecting the definition of the underlying concept the research is concerned with, the more valid a measure is. One of the difficulties of social science is that there is never any clear way of directly assessing **validity.** For example, the IQ test is a measure that might be used reliably by many researchers attempting to quantify intelligence. However,

[7]Edward G. Carmines and Richard Zeller, *Reliability and Validity Assessment.* Sage University Paper Series on Quantitative Applications in the Social Sciences, no. 17 (Beverly Hills, CA.: Sage Publications, 1979).

it will always be debatable just how accurately this test measures a concept as rich, varied, and powerful as intelligence. IQ tests might be reliable, but are they entirely valid?

Improperly conceived measurement is dangerous precisely because it can be so powerful. A tragic and repugnant example was the use of "body counts" as a key to "progress" in the U.S. effort in the Vietnam War. Newscasts about the war would usually report the military's figures on how many "enemies" were killed each day. The implication was that the more we killed, the faster we would win the war. There were two things wrong with this quantified measurement.

First, it didn't measure what some policy makers alleged it measured: the amount of success or failure in achieving overall objectives in the war. Since the war was at least as much a political and psychological struggle as a military conflict, the body counts were largely useless as an index of success. They might have told the military something about the condition of the enemy, but reliance on them promoted adverse political and psychological effects in the Vietnamese population and in our own. The Vietnamese began to notice that it was mainly people of their own race and nationality who were being killed by Americans, regardless of whatever else the war was about. Americans thus came to be feared rather than welcomed as allies by many Vietnamese. At the same time, we began to see ourselves as technological warriors wreaking havoc in a poor country.

A second flaw in the measurement was its implementation. Troops in the field were supposed to count enemy dead and report the number. However, several factors intervened: the confusion (sometimes deliberate) about who was the enemy, the error introduced by having more than one person counting in a particular location, and the chain-of-command pressures for a high body count. Consequently, while the body counts kept going up and led to predictions of success in the war, the actual situation deteriorated.[8]

---

[8]During the Persian Gulf War in 1991, the allied military command avoided these problems by not announcing estimates of Iraqi casualties.

The very important point is that sloppy or inappropriate measurement is generally worse than no measurement at all. Interpreting the results of measurement requires an understanding of the measurement itself. In Chapter 5, we explore the practical steps involved in making and interpreting measurements.

The Hypothesis

Although much of the preceding discussion may have seemed like a serial review of bits and pieces of scientific thinking, a discussion of hypotheses will bring these matters together.

A **hypothesis** is a sentence of a particularly well-cultivated breed. The purpose of a hypothesis is to organize a study. If the hypothesis is carefully formed, all the steps of the scientific method follow, as does an outline for the project, a bibliography, a list of resources needed, and a specification of the measures appropriate to the study. The hypothesis provides the structure.

A hypothesis proposes a relationship between two or more variables. For example: Political participation INCREASES with education. This simple assertion can be seen as a hypothesis. It has a subject (the variable, political participation), a connective verb (a relationship, INCREASES), and an object (the variable, education).

To illustrate the point further:

> Alienation INCREASES with poverty.
> Union members are MORE LIKELY than nonunion members to vote Democratic.

Or, less obviously (and, for exercise, you can identify the variables and relations):

> Absence makes the heart grow fonder.
> An apple a day keeps the doctor away.
> Early to bed, early to rise, makes people healthy, wealthy and wise.

It is crucial to realize that a hypothesis is a supposition, as the Oxford English Dictionary points out, "which serves as a starting point for further investigation by which it may be proved or disproved. . . ." A hypothesis stands near the beginning, not the end, of a study, although good studies may suggest new paths of fruitful inquiry and new hypotheses.

So far, most of our examples of hypotheses have been quite simple. But to go from the straightforward to the bizarre, let us cite an experience in teaching scientific thinking. A student came to one of us with the following proposal for research:

> The fragile psycho-pathological type of double helical existence issuing from the precarious relationship of the colonizer and the colonized (which figuratively is similar to the relationship of Siamese twins) and their respective interaction within the colonial situation is psychologically effective, which ramifications lead to psychological maladjustments, i.e., neuroses which subsequently define the nature of the political particulars therein.

That was just the beginning of the proposal! In all that confusing language, there are lots of variables and many relationships. Sorting it out, however, yields two hypotheses:

> Colonialism IS ASSOCIATED WITH neurotic behavior by colonizer and colonial.
> This neurotic behavior influences the political structure of colonialism.

These two hypotheses, large as they are, were somewhat manageable. The concept *colonialism* describes a well-established political situation. The relationship IS ASSOCIATED WITH was a retreat from saying CAUSES—a precaution taken in view of the limited research resources available to the student. *Neurotic behavior* is a tricky concept, but it has parentage in the literature of psychoanalytic theory; there are behaviors that can respectably be labeled neurotic. From there it becomes a matter of showing the links between the kinds of neurotic, self-destructive behavior that occur in colonial situations and the repressive and authoritarian patterns of colonial politics.

Had the student accomplished all that these hypotheses imply by way of evidence gathering, measurement, and evaluation, he would have been in line for a Ph.D. As long as we both knew that he was just scratching the surface, his paper (bravely entitled "Colonialism: A Game for Neurotics") was good enough for undergraduate requirements.

One of the things this example illustrates is that there is often a prior step to hypothesis formation. The step is called **problem reformulation.** In the preceding example, we began with a generalized concern about colonialism and neurosis. The student elaborated that concern into a complex description of the problem. We narrowed it down by specifying variables and relationships into something that could be dealt with, at least in a general way. With a workable reformulation, defining the ways that variables are represented becomes easier.

One of the arts of social science is skillful problem reformulation. Reformulation requires, in addition to some analytic common sense, the ability to see the variables in a situation and the possible relationship between them. A good first step is to break the problem into its component variables and relationships. Writing down lists of hypotheses associated with a problem enables you to select the ones that answer two questions: Which hypotheses are crucial to the solution of the whole problem? For which hypotheses is there information within the range of your resources? Sometimes these questions force some unpleasant choices, but they help prevent arriving at the end of a research effort with nothing substantial on which to hang a conclusion. The preceding example on colonialism and neurosis illustrates the point.

The importance of establishing a hypothesis correctly before starting off on a research task can hardly be overstated.

The following rules will help:

1. The *variables* must be clearly specified and measurable by some technique you know how to use.
2. The *relationship* between the variables must be precisely stated and measurable.

3. The hypothesis should be *testable* so that evidence of the relationship can be observed, demonstrated, or falsified.

If these rules are not followed, the hypothesis may be unwieldy, ridiculous, or just too hard to research in view of available resources. Precise definitions and thoughtful specification of measurements are, in short, the keys. The struggle to form a hypothesis carefully may not be enjoyable, but the questions raised in the process have to be answered sooner or later.

The hypothesis, then, provides the structure for your entire research effort, whether it involves interviews and surveys, analysis of previously collected data, library research, or all three. It will direct you to relevant information so you do not waste time and effort. The variables you have selected can be researched through library search engines, the Internet, book indexes, periodical guides online services, and CD-ROM/computer database searches. The relationships proposed between the variables suggest the measurement tools and standards for evaluation that you will need to use. The results of the hypothesis test are the substance of your conclusions.

Once relationships between variables have been established through hypothesis formation and testing, these relationships can be expressed as **generalizations.** Generalizations based on tested relationships are the object of science. A generalization is a hypothesis affirmed by testing. As generalizations in a field of study accumulate, they form the raw stuff of theories. But this gets us ahead of the story. For now, we need to see how the scientific method sets the procedure for research into a logical sequence.

The Scientific Method

The technique known as the **scientific method** is quite commonsensical. The model inquiry proceeds by steps that include the following:

1. The identification of the *variables* to be studied
2. A *hypothesis* about the relation of one variable to another or to a situation

3. An *reality test* whereby changes in the variables are measured to see if the hypothesized relationship is evidenced
4. An *evaluation* in which the measured relationship between the variables is compared with the original hypothesis, and *generalizations* about the findings are developed
5. *Suggestions* about the theoretical significance of the findings, factors involved in the test that may have distorted the results, and other hypotheses that the inquiry brings to mind

Although we have sketched here the bare bones of the scientific method, the actual procedure of research does not always start directly with hypothesis formation. As a preliminary to stating hypotheses, social scientists often examine the data collected in a subject area to see if there are connections between the variables. The relationships brought to light by various statistical processes frequently suggest the hypotheses it would be fruitful to explore. Occasionally, simply getting involved with a set of data triggers an interesting thought, a chance insight, or a new idea. A great quantity of data has been generated over the past few decades, so researchers can usually avoid having to begin at the beginning with every inquiry. The analysis of existing data can be extremely helpful in identifying new data needed to test a crucial relationship.

This is only an outline of the scientific method. In the hands of a skilled analyst, other elements are introduced, such as the use of alternative forms of measuring results, detailed conceptual analysis of the variable description, relationships between one's own study and others, assessments of the validity of the measuring instruments, the use of experimental and control groups, and, equally important, careful conjecture that goes beyond what is established in the test itself. These embellishments on the methodology, however, relate more to the tools used in carrying on the method than to the method itself.

The point is that *the scientific method seeks to test thoughts against observable evidence in a disciplined manner, with each step in the process made explicit.*

Consider the differences between two kinds of studies: (1) an empirical scientific study in which the author states his or her values, forms hypotheses, lays out a testing procedure, carefully selects and discusses measurements, produces a specific result, and relates this to the hypotheses; and (2) a nonscientific study in which the author expresses values, develops a general thesis, examines relevant examples, and states the conclusions.

Notice that the tension between thought and investigation is present in both studies. But one important difference is the feasibility of checking the validity of the conclusions in the first example as opposed to the second, by repeating the study. **Replication** is the word social scientists use to indicate the ability to repeat a study as a way of checking on its validity. Replication constitutes a very strong test of a good study because it can reveal errors that might have crept in through the procedures and evaluative judgments contained in the principal study.

A second difficulty with a nonscientific study lies in the problem of relating one study to another. Have you ever been annoyed in a discussion when someone asks you to "define your terms"? Have you ever gotten into arguments that end with, "How do you know that is true?"

A good scientific study presents all the information needed to see what took place. For example, if standard variable definitions are used, a study of voters' assessments of candidates can be added to studies of how voters view issues, parties, or what-ever. As scientists try to build cumulative bodies of knowledge, different studies of the same variables using different measures can be compared to see if measurement techniques create alternative results. The point, once again, is science regulates and specifies the relationship between thought and investigation in such a way that others may know exactly what has been done.

The Many Roles of Theory

Science rests its claim to authority upon its firm basis in observable evidence about something called "reality." We have occasionally described science as, simply, reality testing. Since everybody thinks he or she knows what reality is, science acquires a fundamental appeal. Yet the necessary partner of realism in science is that wholly imaginary phenomenon, **theory**. Without the many roles that theory plays, there would be no science (and, some would argue, there would be no understandable "reality", either).

Just as language arises out of the experience of coming to grips with human needs, so also does theory arise from tasks that people face. The hardest task is to explain what's really going on out there. Volumes have been written about what theory is and isn't. For our purposes, a theory is a set of related propositions that suggest why events occur in the manner that they do.

The propositions that make up theories are of the same form as hypotheses: they consist of concepts and the linkages or relationships between them. Theories are built up as hypotheses are tested and new relationships emerge.

Theory abounds in the most ordinary transactions of life. There are theories of everything from the payoff of slot machines to the inner meaning of *Dilbert* cartoons. The grandest theories of all are religious and philosophical, embracing huge orders of questions about the origin of the physical universe, the history of the species, the purposes of life, and the norms of behavior that lead to virtue and, possibly, happiness. To the faithful, such theories are made true by a belief in supernatural phenomena. These kinds of theories are presented as if they were embedded in the larger cosmos of our existence, awaiting our arrival at understanding.

Social science, by contrast, generally operates from a different perspective on theory. The most conventional posture of a social scientist is one of pragmatism: a theory is only as good as its present and potential uses in explaining observations. The point of any science is to develop a set of theories to explain the events within their range of observation.

It is tempting, but misleading, to conceive of theory as something rocklike and immobile behind the whiz and blur of daily experience. Rather, theory is a sometimes ingenious creation of human beings in their quest for understanding. People create theories in proportion to needs, and the theories they create can be either functional or dysfunctional to those needs. A theory could contain a complete system of categories and generalizations—but still be useless. If, for example, one were to categorize the world in terms of tall things and short things and characterize all the relationships between them, a theory would have been born, but it would be one of dubious utility—not false, but useless.

Social science theory is often derived from fundamental assumptions about human behavior. *Rational actor* theories suggest that individuals, organizations, and nation-states are motivated by a desire to maximize their material interests. Based on this type of theory, we might hypothesize that voters select candidates that further their own economic interest. Alternatively, *psychological* theories assume that voting actions are determined by people's long-term feelings of attachment for political parties. Voters are thought to be socialized, via the family, to be loyal to a particular party. From this theory, we might hypothesize that voters act like their parents, or that they select candidates of the same party year after year. The origins of wars have been explained by rational actor theories and psychological theories, as well as by Marxian theories and other forms of social theory.

We have been discussing what theory is and is not. The next question is: What does it do? The answer is: many things. We list four particular uses of theory in social scientific thinking:

1. Theory provides *patterns* for the interpretation of data.
2. Theory *links* one study with another.
3. Theory supplies frameworks within which concepts and variables acquire *substantive significance*.
4. Theory allows us to interpret the *larger meaning* of our findings for ourselves and others.

Let's illustrate these four uses of theory by looking at the question of voter participation. The rate of voter participation is an important indicator of democracy. It is reasonable to expect that different types of election rules will affect how many people think it is worth their time and effort to vote. We will show how theory influences the way we look at questions of political participation under contrasting sets of election rules. The *patterns* observed in the data, the *links* established between studies, the *substantive significance* of the findings, and their *larger meaning* are all shaped by the theories the researcher uses.

In this illustration, we will focus on how election rules translate people's votes into seats for parties in a legislature. In the United States, nearly all elections are for "single-member districts. "These rules award a single seat to the candidate who wins the most votes in each district. Where the rules allow a wider variety of parties to win seats (as in proportional representation [PR] systems), presumably more people will vote.[9] In PR systems, each party wins a *proportion* of the total number of seats based on its percentage of the vote. Thus, if ten legislative seats are to be allocated in an election, most of the seats would likely go to candidates from large parties, but smaller parties can elect candidates to one or two seats by winning 10 or 20 percent of the vote.

Some theorize that winner-take-all rules in single-member districts might reduce participation. In the United States, the rules mean that nearly all seats are won by candidates from the Democratic and Republican parties. The hypothesis would be that citizens who are not oriented toward candidates from the major parties might be discouraged about voting.[10] Since a large slice of the electorate see themselves as "independents," this becomes an important factor in assessing the effectiveness of U.S. democracy.

Consider the data presented in Table 2.2. The table shows the average level of turnout for elections held in various countries under three types of election rules. *Winner-take-all* rules

[9]See, for example, G. Bingham Powell, "American Voter Turnout in Comparative Perspective," *American Political Science Review* 80, no. 1 (1986), pp. 17–43.

[10]One study attempted to hold cultural differences constant by comparing turnout in US local elections that used winner-take-all to those using "semi-proportional" elections. It found that 'semi-PR' systems increased turnout by about 5 per cent. See Shaun Bowler, David Brockington and Todd Donovan, "Election Systems and Voter Turnout: Experiments in the United States," *Journal of Politics*, 63, no. 3, (2001), pp. 902–915.

TABLE 2.2   TURNOUT IN NATIONAL ELECTIONS, 1990s

	Type of Election Rules for National Legislature		
	Winner-take-all[a]	Proportional[b]	Mixed[c]
Average turnout	66.5%	74.3%	77.3%
Standard deviation	9.4	11.3	3.8
Number of nations	4	3	12

[a] Canada, Great Britain, France, and United States
[b] Germany, Japan, New Zealand
[c] Denmark, Finland, Greece, Iceland, Ireland, Israel, Netherlands, Norway, Portugal, Spain, Sweden, Switzerland.

NOTE: Average turnout for national elections held in 19 advanced industrialized democracies where voting is largely non-compulsory.

SOURCE: Authors' calculations from raw data listed in Russell J. Dalton, *Citizen Politics: Public Opinion and Political Parties in Advanced Industrial Democracies* (Chatham, N.J.: Chatham House, 2002), p. 36.

award seats only to candidates that finish first in a single district. *Proportional* systems typically allow voters to select a party's slate of candidates, then allocate multiple seats roughly proportionate to each party's vote share. Some nations elect part of their legislature with winner-take-all rules, and the rest with proportional rules. These nations have *mixed* systems.

What is the message of these data? Looking at the top row of data, we find that election rules might affect participation in national elections. Countries that use PR averaged 74 percent turnout, compared with a 66 percent turnout rate for the nations that used winner-take-all rules. These data are averages based on elections in different countries. The data suggest, but do not prove directly, that proportional representation influences more citizens to vote. However, rival explanations and intervening variables, such as cultural differences, might explain these patterns as well.[11]

[11] Douglas Amy, *Real Choices, New Voices*. (Cambridge, England: Cambridge University Press, 1993), pp. 140–153; Arend Lijphart, "Unequal Participation: Democracy's Unresolved Dilemma," *American Political Science Review* 91, no. 1 (1997), pp. 1–14.

Where does the theory enter in? What theories fit this *pattern* of data? One theory is that people are more likely to act—in this case, to vote—when they think their action will have tangible consequences. In other words, they're more likely to vote if they think their most preferred party might win, or if they think their vote might make a difference in a close election. Thus PR systems might attract followers of smaller parties to vote because of the greater likelihood that their vote could have the effect of electing a representative. Since PR allows more parties in a legislature, the data in Table 2.1 seem to support the theory that PR mobilizes a wider range of citizens because their vote is more likely to have a tangible result.

Another theory proposes that people vote out of a sense of "civic duty." Under this theory, they vote regardless of perceptions about their preferred party's chances of winning seats.[12] Since we have no data about how the public's sense of civic duty varies across these nations, the fact that our data are consistent with one theory does not mean that we can reject the rival theory.

Being aware of different theories allows social scientists to *link* their studies with previous research. It also provides a means to generate additional tests that might allow us to reject rival theories that offer alternative explanations for patterns seen in the data. If we found, for example, that there were no differences in perceived 'civic duty' among the places reflected in the data in Table 2.1, a stronger case could be made that PR motivates more people to vote than winner-take-all elections.

PR might cause the perceived benefits of voting (greater chances of representation) to outweigh the costs. It might be that nonvoters in the United States are those who feel politically marginalized by electoral institutions that prevent their preferred

---

[12]For a discussion of these rival theories, see Donald Green and Ian Shapiro, *Pathologies of Rational Choice Theory* (New Haven, Conn.: Yale University Press, 1994). Cf. Kristen Monroe, *The Heart of Altrusim: Perceptions of a Common Humanity* (Princeton, N.J.: Princeton University Press, 1996).

candidates from winning office. Through these links in reasoning, social scientists can accumulate knowledge of relationships between different theoretical constructs. So far we have seen two uses of theory in relation to the example in Table 2.1: the *patterns* the theory provides, and the ways that theory *links* one study to another.

The third use of theory is now apparent. We need to assess the *substantive significance* of what is observed here.[13] That is, we need to ask if the observations have implications that are interesting or important. This result could be important for testing the usefulness of "rational action" theories in explaining political behavior. In this case, we might infer that a switch to PR rules could boost turnout by 10 percent in a nation using winner-take-all.[14]

It would seem that giving people more choices in elections might lead to greater citizen participation. This raises a host of interesting substantive questions: How would the participation of these voters change a political system? What new parties might succeed? How would institutions such as Congress function with several parties?

The *larger meaning* of these findings for theories relating political institutions to human behavior lies beyond these specific substantive questions. Participation in a representative democracy is not just a matter of having the formal right to vote. People are also sensitive to the results of the process and to the constraints that institutions create. Clearly, other factors are involved, but it would seem that election systems that lead to the representation of more social groups also encourage more people to vote. Proportional rules that produce representation for a wider variety of

---

[13]This should not be confused with statistical significance (See Chapter 5), which tells whether the difference between winner-take-all and PR elections may have occurred by chance. Substantive significance relates to theory rather than to statistical probability.

[14]Comparative studies that account for additional variables suggest that the independent effect of PR on turnout varies between 3 and 7 percent. See Andre Blais and Agnieszka Dobrzynska, "Turnout in Electoral Democracies," *European Journal of Political Research* 18 (1998), pp. 167–181; Andres Lander and Henry Milner, "Do Voters Turn Out More under Proportional Than Majoritarian Systems?," *Electoral Studies,* 18 (1999), pp. 235–250.

people are also likely to have broader effects on citizens' attitudes about politics and government generally.[15]

In discussing theory, we have presented an illustration of its uses in social scientific research. Most researchers are intent on proving their theory to be "right." However, Karl Popper, an influential analyst of the social sciences, shows us that the best use of science is often to refute theories rather than to "prove" them:

> Of nearly every theory it may be said that it agrees with many facts: this is one of the reasons why a theory can be said to be corroborated only if we are unable to find refuting facts, rather than if we are able to find supporting facts.[16]

In other words, data may be more impressive as evidence for the theories they refute than for the theories they support.

What we have not captured in this discussion of theory is the subtlety and creativity with which people think about what they are observing. Theory illuminates observations. Yet, like a beam of light playing on an object, every theory leaves shadows that challenge our imaginations.

On one hand, we can only say that without theory, social science would be an incoherent and meaningless pile of observations, data, and statistics. On the other hand, not all social science can be tied to rigorous and specific theoretical formulations. However, it is absolutely clear that complex social problems need all the well-informed study we can develop. The organization and evaluation of that knowledge in theoretical form is almost as important as gathering it in the first place. History is littered with the wreckage of poorly conceived social theories—sometimes with tragic results—though the power of theoretical imagination has been responsible for some of civilization's greatest advances.

---

[15]C. Anderson and C. Guilloty, "Political Institutions and Satisfaction with Democracy: A Cross-National Analysis of Consensus and Majoritarian System," *American Political Science Review* 91, no 1 (1997), pp. 68–81.

[16]In *Popper Selections,* ed. David Miller (Princeton, N.J.: Princeton University Press, 1985), p. 437.

We now have in hand the basic tools of scientific thinking. But tools, by themselves, don't get the job done. We need a plan or, as described in the next chapter, a *strategy* for putting those tools to work to produce some knowledge.

● CONCEPTS INTRODUCED

Concept	Hypothesis
Variable	Problem reformulation
Discrete quantification	Generalization
Continuous quantification	Scientific method
Measurement	Replication
Reliability	Theory
Validity	

● QUESTIONS FOR DISCUSSION

1. Consider the concept *unemployment*.
   a. How can it be given a definition so that it can be measured as a variable?
   b. How many definitions of unemployment can you think of?
   c. How do these definitions differ?

2. Evaluate different measures of unemployment in terms of reliability and validity.
   a. In terms of reliability, if other researchers used your measures (variables), would they produce similar results?
   b. In terms of validity, do the measures do a good job of representing the concept *umemployment*?

3. Consider the data about religion and voting in the 1996 election. Develop a table that expresses the relationship between the two variables. Can you form hypotheses about how (or why) religion is associated with voting?

4. One of the more complex questions that social scientists deal with is: Why do people rebel against their governments?

Consider three examples of major revolutions (seventeenth-century England, eighteenth-century France, early-twentieth-century Russia). Based on these examples, can you form some hypotheses about why revolutions occur? When forming your hypotheses, consider the following:

a. What variables are associated with the occurrence of revolutions?
b. How do you define concepts such as *revolution*?
c. Is your definition something that other researchers could apply reliably to other nations in which revolutions have or have not occurred?
d. How are the variables in your hypotheses linked together?
e. How would you test the hypotheses?
f. Would another person reach the same conclusion as you if he or she used your measures and the tests you suggest?

PREVIEW OF CHAPTER THREE

- Thinking Over the Problem
  - Focus
  - Hypothesis Formation
  - Operationalizing Concepts
- Reality Testing
  - Organizing the Bibliography
  - Doing Research
  - Analyzing the Results
- Understanding the Results
  - Evaluating Concept Operationalization and Variable
  - Measurement
  - Were the Measures Any Good?
  - Can Statistics Be Trusted?
  - How Do Your Findings Fit with Theories in the Field?

Chapter THREE

STRATEGIES

> "A fact is like a sock
> which doesn't stand up
> when it is empty. In
> order that a fact may
> stand up, one has to put
> into it the reason and the
> feeling which have caused
> it to exist."
>
> –LUIGI PIRANDELLO

Observant readers will notice that two words, usually thought to be integral to the scientific method, rarely appear in this book. They are *fact* and *truth*. What both words have in common is an air of absolutism that misleads those who become involved in the scientific approach to learning. *Fact* means, according to its word root, "a thing done." That things do get done is not disputed, but the trouble is that "things done" are perceived not by some neutral omnipotent observer, but by people.

People have limited powers of perception and structures of instinct and interest that influence how they see the world. *Science is a process for making*

these perceptions as explicit and open to examination as possible.
But the results of scientific procedure must always be taken as
just that—an *attempt* to control a process that our very humanity
makes difficult, if not impossible, to control totally.

For working purposes, social scientists generally regard a
fact as "a particular ordering of reality in terms of a theoretical
interest."[1] Anything identified as a fact is tied to the particular
interests the observer brings to the study of the phenomenon.
Further than that we cannot usefully go, for a philosophical forest
looms in which subtle questions are raised about whether a
tree that falls unobserved has really fallen, since we can't know
that it did.

The term **truth** is red meat for philosophers, and they are
welcome to it. Science prefers to operate in the less lofty region
of **falsifiable statements** that can be checked by someone else.
Every good scientific proposition or generalization is stated in
such a way that subsequent observations may provide either
supporting evidence or evidence that raises questions about the
accuracy of the proposition. By making the degree of verification
a permanent consideration in science, a good many rash conclusions can be avoided.

"What, then, are we to believe in?" might be the response to
this noncommittal attitude toward fact and truth. If you want
something absolute to believe in, it must be found outside of
science. Science is a working procedure for answering questions
through the refinement of experience. Scientists may develop
theories of awe-inspiring power, but the way such theories meet
our very human needs for belief is a personal matter separate
from the meaning of science for inquiry. To "believe in science"
means no more or less than to be committed to judgments based
on observations that can be replicated, rather than on some other
kind of evidence or mental process.

You are now familiar with basic elements of science, such as
variables, measurements, and hypotheses. In this chapter we will
concentrate on how to shape ideas about the world into a form

[1]David Easton, *The Political System* (New York: Knopf, 1953), p. 53.

that allows for reality testing. Then the process of reality testing will be broken down into its parts. Finally, we will see what evaluative steps need to be taken for understanding the results of research.

The following remarks are designed as a step-by-step guide to scientific analysis. However, it must be realized that we are trying to capture only the most significant aspects of scientific procedure, not the finer points or the intricacies that a sophisticated researcher would want to introduce. The following chapter, entitled "Refinements," adds to each element some ideas for increasing the power of your research strategy.

Please bear in mind that all we are doing here is regulating what is natural to human thought: a tension between thought and reality testing. So this chapter is organized into three sections: Thinking Over the Problem, Reality Testing, and Understanding the Results.

Thinking Over the Problem

The biggest challenge in doing research occurs at the very beginning. Once you have met that challenge, other steps fall into place. This is the problem of limiting the topic, or, more positively, of selecting an approach to the topic that will most efficiently get at the thing you want to understand. Most students have had the experience of writing a long, rambling, poorly focused paper. As the need for conclusions looms with the final pages, there occasionally arises the awful feeling that no firm conclusion can be reached based on the evidence presented. The reason for such an inglorious end usually can be found in the beginning.

Focus

Since most of us are not trained to think in terms of formulating our ideas into hypotheses and testing them, it is best to start writing things down in the way they occur to the mind: as a sequence of ideas, thoughts, and notions. Ask yourself, "Why am I interested in this? What is it that I am really after?" See what happens. You might start with a broad topic:

> This country is in big trouble. Most people don't think that politics matters these days—they don't want to have anything to do with it. Politics is such a joke.

Big subjects, but there is a theme here about whether modern democracy works.

At this stage it is a good idea to try to capture these thoughts in a paragraph or two. Get it on paper! Some general reading is a good idea. It helps to map out the areas of investigation. Too much reading may be a bad idea. Don't try to get into your actual research until you have thought through the larger frame of the problem.

Suppose you wind up with two paragraphs like this:

> Something has changed in America. In the old days, it seemed like more people believed that they could make a difference in things. Maybe they thought that government could make society better, or maybe they just had more free time.

> Today, most of the people I talk to don't care about politics and they don't trust the government. Who's got the time to get involved with politics? Besides, unless you have money to contribute, they won't listen to you.

These paragraphs actually contain a number of concepts and variables, a network of relationships, and a whole series of hypotheses. But at least there is some indication of the possibilities for a more focused study.

At this point, two levels of study could be mounted: *descriptive* and *relational*. A **descriptive study** collects information about a situation. One might describe an institution, event, or behavior, or some combination of these. Good description is the beginning of science. Leonardo da Vinci's masterful notes and drawings of human anatomy enabled generations of medical scientists to advance their understanding of the body. Some specialized descriptive studies analyze information about a single variable—for example, the breakdown of families. What does it consist of? How much of it is going on? How have things changed over time? When does it occur most frequently? These studies are valuable sources for higher forms of analysis.

Relational analysis examines connections between things. The basic form consists of probing the links between one variable and another: the relation between trust and being involved with politics, for example, or the relationship between age and having a sense that participation matters. A series of relational studies can form the basis for causal analysis, that special type of relational study in which the most powerful of connections between variables is isolated.

The initial thoughts on the topic given in the preceding paragraphs seem to imply a whole series of relations. If you are impatient to get to the root of the situation, a relational analysis of some aspect of the general problem of participation and trust might be the next step.

Hypothesis Formation

With the topic narrowed somewhat, hypothesis formation becomes easier. The question is twofold: What are the essential variables? What are the relations between them? One intriguing element of our sample problem involves two variables: political participation and trust. The paragraphs that were written suggest a link between the two. What is the nature of the link? What word expresses that relationship? If we leave aside causal analysis, the suggested relationship is a simple one: People are more likely to participate in politics if they are trusting, or if they think it will make some difference.

Even with all these words, we still boil things down to two variables and one relationship: participation IS ASSOCIATED WITH trust. Most studies, of course, contain several hypotheses, possibly interconnected as elements of one large thesis. But for purposes of illustration we will stay with something less demanding.

Operationalizing Concepts

To *operationalize* a concept means to put it in a form that permits some kind of measurement of variation. In Chapter Two we discussed turning concepts into usable variables; this process is called **operationalization**. Translating a concept into something that allows the observation of variation is a tricky process. If it is done properly, two conditions will be met: (1) the operational version will fit the meaning of the original concept as closely as possible (*validity*); (2) the measurement(s) of variation can be replicated by others (*reliability*).

How does one operationalize whether people are engaged in political activity? Well, how about asking people some simple questions about *political participation:*

- *Did you go to any political meetings, rallies, or speeches?*
- *Did you do any work for a political party or candidate?*
- *Have you ever written a letter to a newspaper about a public matter?*
- *Did you vote in the last election, or did something keep you from voting?*

Once the answers are given, it then becomes a matter of identifying patterns in the responses to individual questions, or evaluating how responses to the set of questions hold together. We can look at the responses and see if any themes or trends emerge. However we approach it, responses should give us clues about how many people are politically active.

Trends in responses to these questions about *political participation* can also help us assess our research question. If these questions have been asked over a long period of time, we can see if people are more or less engaged with politics today. The variable *trust in government* is often measured with responses to this question:

> How much of the time do you think you can trust the government in Washington to do what is right—just about always, most of the time, or only some of the time?

Looking back at the preceding paragraphs, we see that the main hypothesis is about how low levels of *trust* might make people less likely to be engaged with politics today. Normative theories of democracy suggest that a healthy polity needs both some minimal level of both trust, and some minimal level of public participation in the political process.

At this point, we will observe the research strategy actually used in studies by Robert Putnam, a Harvard political scientist. A condensed version of one of Putnam's articles, "Tuning In and Turning Out: The Strange Disappearance of Social Capital in America," is reprinted as Appendix A in this book.[2]

Putnam offers us the idea that low levels of political participation are due, in part, to a decline in membership in social groups. Putnam draws from the works of Alexis de Tocqueville—an early observer of American society—and contemporary sociologist James Coleman to develop his theory and hypotheses.[3] He argues that people are less engaged with politics today than they were in the 1950s because they lack trust.

Membership in voluntary social groups is expected to somehow transform people, making them more politically engaged and build "civic capacity" essential for democracy.[4] Americans from older generations, the theory goes, are more active in certain groups that build social trust and social connections. Today, people may be less likely to know their neighbors, and less likely to interact with friends.[5] Such connections allow them to see the

---

[2]Robert D. Putnam, "Tuning In and Tuning Out: The Strange Disappearance of Social Capital in America," *PS: Political Science and Politics,* 28, no. 4, (1995), 664–683. See also another article by Putnam, "Bowling Alone: America's Declining Social Capital," *Journal of Democracy,* 6, no. 1 (1995), 65–78.

[3]See James Coleman, "Social Capital in the Creation of Human Capital," *American Journal of Sociology,* 94S: 95-S120 (1988).

[4]Another observer wrote that the "interpersonal transformation" that comes from being in groups "cannot be easily measured with the blunt instruments of social science." Jane Mansbridge, "On the Idea that Participation Makes Better Citizens," in *Citizen Competence and Democratic Institutions,* eds. Stephen Elkin and Karol Soltan (University Park: Pennsylvania State University Press, 1999), 291.

[5]Robert Putnam, *Bowling Alone: The Collapse and Revival of American Community* (New York: Simon and Schuster, 2000).

usefulness of "cooperation for mutual benefit." To oversimplify the argument, a decline in social activity has caused a decline in trust and political activity. If we don't join groups like the PTA or bowling leagues, we don't learn to trust each other. We thus fail to learn how any collective effort, like politics, makes any difference. Putnam and others refer to the sum of the social connections, norms, and social trust that we get from group activity as **social capital**.[6] Coleman defines social capital as the social connections between individuals that "facilitate action."[7]

Read Putnam's article in Appendix A; it will enhance your understanding as we explore how his research was done. The article is an example of a carefully presented summary of a larger research project. The author begins by discussing the theoretical background of the work, the steps taken in generating and testing hypothesis, and the larger meaning of his results. This is a model to follow—even for a brief research paper.

In operationalizing the variable *political participation,* Putnam examined answers to several questions, including those listed above. He is also interested in how the decline in political participation is associated with *trust,* and with *social capital.* Social capital, like many concepts in the social sciences, does not provide us an immediately obvious means for operationalization—it's not something we can see or count directly. It's a big concept, and Putnam's theory offers us guidance about what to look for. He suggests that social capital is produced by membership in social groups. This means that one indirect measure of social capital can be answers to simple questions about the social groups a person might join.

Putnam operationalized *social capital* as social group memberships. He uses responses to survey questions as one of his instruments to measure group membership. His theory leads him to use membership in the following groups as indicators of social capital:

[6]Putnam, 666.

[7]James Coleman, *Foundations of Social Theory* (Cambridge, MA: Belknap, 1990), 304.

TABLE 3.1   VOLUNTARY GROUP MEMBERSHIP IN 14 NATIONS

Nation	Sports Group/Club	Church-related Group	Arts or Literary Group/Club
Belgium	21.9%	8.9%	14.0%
Denmark	34.8	20.9	10.3
France	16.1	6.2	6.3
Germany (West)	27.9	15.9	4.9
Great Britain	23.8	19.4	6.8
Greece	6.5	1.8	5.6
Ireland	25.6	17.5	3.8
Italy	10.2	8.8	6.5
Netherlands	35.2	26.9	10.7
New Zealand	47.7	38.9	n/a
Norway	27.2	10.5	8.2
Portugal	11.5	5.6	4.6
Spain	8.3	5.9	3.3
United States	21.6	33.4	9.8

NOTE: Group membership is assumed to be one reflection of levels of social capital. Cell entries are percentages of respondents claiming membership.

SOURCES: Authors' analysis of raw data files—Europe, 1990 Eurobaromerter Survey 34.0; New Zealand, 1999 New Zealand Election Study; USA, 1994 General Social Survey.

- Church-related groups
- Sports groups (soccer teams, softball leagues, bowling leagues)
- Arts or literary societies (theater groups, choirs)
- Labor unions
- Fraternal organizations (Lions, Elks, Masons, Jaycees)
- Service clubs
- Civic organizations (Boy Scouts, Red Cross, PTA)

Table 3.1 illustrates how frequently people mentioned being members of some of these groups. Although Putnam is concerned primarily with trends in the United States, these descriptive data show that Americans join social groups at rates that match or exceed those in many other democratic nations. Now, having operationalized the key variable *social capital* in terms of group membership, the stage is set for organizing the whole inquiry.

Reality Testing

Organizing the Bibliography

With a hypothesis in mind, it is a good idea to do some additional reading before actually beginning research. This will help you check your formulation of hypotheses and operationalization of variables against other efforts. Use a library database or the Internet to do a search on variables in the hypothesis. Articles, books, and Web sites are all valuable sources for information and background. Often a single journal article on the topic will contain footnotes and a bibliography that can guide you to most of the significant literature on the subject. A more sophisticated researcher would take this step first—it can save a lot of time in the thinking-it-over stage. However, beginning students often come to problems of social analysis "fresh."

Doing Research

Many students might not think of mounting the kind of research enterprise suggested here. The survey data we present here are publicly available via the Internet for analysis if you wish to pursue this further.[8] The following examples are for instructional purposes, however, and should be sufficient to show how social science research works so that your own project can be formulated with the clearest possible strategy.

Robert Putnam and others working in this area tested their hypotheses by reanalyzing surveys that had already been done. A lot of social science is carried on in this way. As researchers look at "old" data with a different perspective and a new hypothesis,

---

[8]The National Election Study Guide to Public Opinion and Electoral Behavior is online at: *http://www.umich.edu/~nes/*. The General Social Survey cumulative file is online at: *http://www.icpsr.umich.edu:8080/GSS/homepage.htm*. The GSS site allows you to do online analysis of the survey data. Data used in Robert Putnam's book can be found at *http://www.bowlingalone.com*.

fresh insights are revealed. In doing your own research, check with faculty members and the library to see if there might be data that you could use to test your hypotheses before you set out to collect your own.

In this case, scholars often look at data in the General Social Survey (GSS)—a major academic survey of American attitudes, opinions, and behavior—to examine how trends in social group membership relate to trends in trust and political participation. This isn't the only data source he uses. He draws from other surveys, and from records that groups keep about their membership.

Based on his theory, Putnam decided in advance that some types of group memberships are more important than others in building trust and political engagement. Religious groups, unions, parent–teacher organizations, civic groups, and fraternal organizations are highlighted—but his data sources provide measures of membership in many other types of groups.

The survey questions that Putnam discusses in his research were asked every year for nearly two decades, which allows him to compare trends in group membership, trust, and political participation. The summary of the responses to these questions reveals some interesting patterns (see Table 3.2) and permits some intriguing observations: for example, some forms of political participation are in decline, but voting appears to remain high. Government records actually show a decline in voter turnout, so can responses to the voting question be trusted?[9] We also see that trust in government has dropped substantially—is the drop in participation related to the decline in trust.

In any case, the results in Table 3.2, while perhaps not too encouraging for American society, do seem to support some of the basic ideas of the study—political participation and trust are both in decline. There is more to concluding a study, however, than simply saying: "See, I was right (or wrong)!"

---

[9]Actual voter turnout in presidential elections hovered around 50 per cent from 1992 to 2000. The NES surveys probably oversample actual voters. At the same time, some actual nonvoters in the sample probably tell interviewers that they voted when, in fact, they did not. We will discuss these issues in Chapter 5.

FIGURE 3.1   TRENDS IN TRUST AND GROUP
MEMBERSHIP 1974–1994

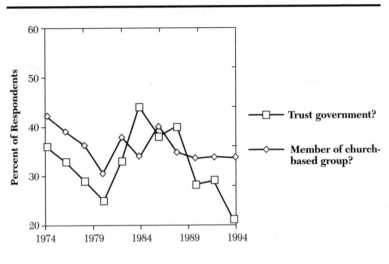

Year of Survey

Analyzing the Results

Results need to be placed in perspective. In this study, the
real issue was whether membership in certain social groups led
people to be more politically engaged and trusting of government. There are many ways we can test for this relationship.
One is to look at trends over time. Figure 3.1 presents some preliminary results from trends in responses to GSS and NES survey
questions. We see that from 1974 to 1994, membership in
church-based groups was in decline (albeit just slightly), and that
trust in government dropped from more than 40 per cent of
respondents in 1974 to 20 per cent in 1994. These results seem
to support the basic hypothesis that social group membership is
related to trusting government—but they must be subjected
to further analysis. As Table 3.2 indicates, trust in government
has actually been fairly constant (and low) since the 1970s. Self-
reported political participation also appears to have dropped
slightly since 1960, but can we be sure that the decline is caused
by a corresponding decline in membership in social groups?

TABLE 3.2   TRENDS IN POLITICAL PARTICIPATION
AND TRUST, 1960–2000

	1960	1968	1976	1984	1988	1996	2000
Attend political meetings, rallies, or speeches?	8%	9%	6%	9%	7%	5%	5%
Work for a political party or candidate?	6	6	5	6	3	2	3
Vote in the last election?	79	76	72	74	70	73	73
Trust government always/most time?	73°	61	33	44	40	33	44

°1958. The question was not asked in 1960.

SOURCE: National Election Study, various years.

Another analytic device is to see what impact other important variables have on the results. Our discussion of social capital theory suggested that membership in social groups has been in decline for some time, and also suggests that recent generations of Americans may be less likely to participate in church groups, service clubs, fraternal organizations, and other such social groups.

The data shown in Table 3.3 seem to bear this out. This table shows the percent of people in different age *cohorts* who are members of no social groups, one or two groups, or three or more groups. Since we are interested in a person's generation more than age, we list when they were born to better illustrate when they reached adulthood.[10] As we can see, respondents who became adults in the 1950s (the "born 1925–1934" and "born 1935–1944" cohorts) were least likely to report that they were not a member of any social group. In fact, 31 per cent of each of these cohorts were members of three or more groups. In contrast, people who became adults in the 1990s (the "born 1965–1974" cohort) were least likely to report having a high number of memberships. They score lowest on the variable that we assume to be measuring social capital.

[10]The table presents "pooled" data from many annual GSS polls. This means that a 20-year-old respondent surveyed in 1972 is placed in the "born 1945–1954" age cohort, while a 20-year-old surveyed in 1992 is placed in the "born 1965–1974" cohort.

TABLE 3.3   LEVELS OF SOCIAL GROUP MEMBERSHIP,
BY AGE COHORT

	AGE COHORT				
Born between:	1925–1934	1935–1944	1945–1954	1955–1964	1965–1974
Turned 18 in about:	1948	1958	1968	1978	1988
Not a member of any group	25%	26%	29%	36%	37%
Member of one or two social groups	44	42	42	39	41
Member of three or more social groups	31	31	29	25	22

SOURCE: Authors' calculations from raw data in GSS 1972–2000 cumulative datafile.

To conclude, there's something going on here: Trust and some forms of political participation are in decline, and the youngest generation of Americans have the lowest levels of social capital. This is consistent with Putnam's theory, but it does not "prove" it. There's much more that can be done to test how these things are related, but we now have a better grip on the problem than when we started.

We want to emphasize that by consulting multiple reality tests, you can gain perspective on the utility of the one you have constructed. At the same time, other studies can provide a general check on your findings.

Understanding the Results

Evaluating Concept Operationalization and Variable Measurement

Now that you have some research experience with the subject, rethink each step of the strategy in light of what happened. There is a big difference between thinking of a way to operationalize a concept and having it work as expected in the process of research.

The following are some questions for this project:

1. Can you be sure that the measures of political participation are valid?
2. Do the groups that we use as indicators of social capital all play the same role in building social connections among people? Is social capital simply an abstraction created by the researchers' interpretation of the data?
3. How can we establish if there is a causal relationship between social group membership and political participation? Between group membership and trust in government? What is the direction of causation?
4. Is the social capital argument something unique to America? Would we expect to find similar patterns in survey data from Europe and elsewhere?

We also need to consider how the survey data might be biased. There is a problem of a person's state of mind in answering a question. Any number of factors can influence responses. For example, female interviewers might produce different responses from women than male interviewers do. It is useful to repeat studies in different times and places. If you ask college students to fill out questionnaires, be ready for the campus wit. The jokers, the devious, and the perverse can foul up a questionnaire in many ways.

Another possible form of interference with honest responses arises from respondents who feel there is something fishy about the project, the researcher, the questions, or the presumed confidentiality of the responses. An erstwhile sophomore once polled the faculty of a church-affiliated college about their personal use of marijuana. She did these interviews in person and assured the faculty that each response would be "confidential"—the data summaries were to be broken down by department and rank, and the final paper would then be placed in the library. However, a junior faculty member in a small department might conceivably have been wary of the promised confidentiality, and might have been less than honest in responding to such an invitation to persecution if not prosecution.

In dealing with people, science does not substitute for savvy.

Were the Measures Any Good?

Self-criticism isn't a particularly welcome task, but in social science it serves two specific purposes. Obviously, it helps to reexamine a project after you've finished to be sure that the steps along the way are sufficiently well done to lead directly to the conclusion. Reexamination serves another function, however. In dealing with something as slippery as the measurement of social phenomena, whatever is learned in the development and use of measures needs to be shared. A measure can look very impressive at the outset of an inquiry. The experience gained in actually using it, however, may turn up some unexpected weaknesses that, if stated as part of the results, can save someone else a lot of work.

In the case of Robert Putnam's social capital project, there are hundreds of different social groups in which people might report membership. In various writings, Putnam emphasizes a different mix of groups that matter—with church, sports, and arts clubs often cited as essential reservoirs of social capital.[11] The specific groups we decide to measure matter because different measures often produce different results. Although Figure 3.1 shows a decline in church-based groups that corresponds with a decline in trust, questions from the same GSS surveys show that membership in other social groups was increasing (sports groups, school fraternities, and professional associations).

So which groups best cultivate the norms, networks, and social connections that are essential to a democratic society? We need to know this in order to know which measures of group membership to use. If sports groups such as bowling leagues are important, we could ask people if they go bowling in leagues. But

[11]See the articles in note 2, as well as Robert Putnam, *Making Democracy Work: Civic Traditions in Modern Italy* (Princeton, NJ: Princeton University Press, 1993), and Robert Putnam, *Bowling Alone: The Collapse and Revival of American Community* (New York: Simon and Schuster, 2000).

would responses to this question really measure how, or if, they interact with their fellow bowlers? Moreover, what does our measure pick up if many of the people who answer "yes" simply took a high school bowling class for P.E.?[12]

Remember that the idea behind social capital is that membership in groups leads to contacts with other people that build trust. A more convincing measure of the effects of social groups may be to ask people about the groups they join, and then also ask them how much time they spend meeting with members of the groups. This might give us a more direct measure of how social groups affect people. The GSS also includes questions about working as a volunteer and hours spent in certain group activities.

Does this criticism invalidate the measure? No; there is no such thing as a perfect measure. The point is to be able to defend your measure against likely alternatives. A researcher must have a good defense of how variables are measured and defined. Comparing findings obtained by different measures and diverse approaches to observation helps build understanding.

Can Statistics Be Trusted?

Assorted mystics throughout the ages have made much of examining the entrails of birds for portents and predictions of the future. Those skilled in statistical criticism are probably the modern heirs of this profession (particularly those who are adept at finding good news and bad news in any given statistic). That statistics do not provide, in and of themselves, precise answers to social inquiries surprises some and comforts others. It is easy to say that statistics can lie, or that they never quite get the whole message across and are therefore useless. But the question is: Statistics (or measurement) compared to what? Compared to language concepts such as "more," "less," "a whole bunch," or

---

[12]The filmmaker Michael Moore noted that mass murderers Eric Harris and Dylan Klebold both took bowling at Columbine High School. Poking a finger at faulty causal reasoning, he suggested, in irony, that bowling might cause mass murder rather than social trust.

"a little bit," statistics can be more precise. It is true that evidence involving numbers can be misleading—but words can mislead too. Symbolic cues, loaded terms, imprecise language—all distort knowledge. The advantage of a scientific approach to observation is that biases can be more easily exposed because the specification of meanings and procedures is so explicit as to permit replication.

Of course, the wrong statistic can be used as easily as the wrong word, and science is no substitute for common sense. As you learn more about statistics, you will find that researchers typically use several statistics to summarize a situation, rather than relying on a single indicator in order to compensate for the faults of any particular statistic.

How Do Your Findings
Fit with Theories in the Field?

Although a simple experiment or inquiry might answer some puzzle that is on your mind, it might also relate in interesting ways to more general issues that are contained within theories of the subject. For example, it is mildly interesting to know how education influences people's judgments of presidential candidates. It is a lot more interesting to fit that finding to a whole set of ideas about the human condition. Can we indeed be trusted to select our own leaders? Does democracy really work? These are large theoretical perspectives, but theory doesn't have to be grand to be good. There are less global theories that explain key pieces of events.

Coleman, Putnam, and others who examine the effects of social capital begin their projects by discussing social and democratic theory, as well as previous research on the relationship between social groups and politics. They cite other writers, including Tocqueville, who speak highly of the "civic" effects of social groups. Tocqueville himself wrote in the 1830s that one of the most important aspects of American democracy was the widespread participation in voluntary associations—social groups that provided forums where people learned skills that made them better democratic citizens. This discussion highlights the relevance of Putnam's study. They show that declining interest in politics may have roots in deep social changes, rather than being due to our current crop of politicians, or contemporary disdain for negative ads.

In evaluating the research we have presented in this chapter, refer to the general readings you have done. Also, if time allows, do some more investigations of what other people have found out about the link between social capital (or social group membership) and engagement with politics. Think about how (or if) democracy could be strengthened if more people interacted with each other in various social settings like charities, neighborhood organizations, sports clubs, and civic groups.

Scientific procedure is lifeless by itself. In the hands of an imaginative researcher it becomes a very useful tool, but the mind is a far more subtle instrument than any set of procedures for investigation. Where science as method ends, scientists as people take over.

A noteworthy scientist once commented that "science is observation," by which he meant to suggest that getting all wound up in the details of experimental and control groups, statistics, and the rest can obscure the purpose of scientific inquiry: using your head to understand what is going on.[13] There is no such thing as the perfect experiment that explains everything about a given phenomenon. Be wary of people who say they have proven something—especially with "facts" based on statistics. Use the scientific method as a critical tool as well as a means of discovery. Seek out vulnerable assumptions and the limitations of evidence so that you know both what has been demonstrated and what has not.[14]

---

[13]Robert Hodes, "Aims and Methods of Scientific Research," Occasional paper no. 9 (New York: American Institute of Marxist Studies, 1968), pp. 11–14.

[14]For examples of questionable uses of science, see Daisie Radner and Michael Radner, *Science and Unreason* (Belmont, Calif.: Wadsworth, 1982).

In relating your work to theory and in speculating about its larger consequences, you have a chance to be imaginative and creative, though not undisciplined or completely fanciful. Charles Fourier, a French socialist, extended the observation that people work better and are happier in communes to the notion that advances in human understanding would cause world history to ascend (through hundreds of years) to a situation so utopian that every day would begin with a parade, the oceans would turn into lemonade, and we would be transported across the seas by friendly whales. That's a bit much.

• CONCEPTS INTRODUCED

Fact	Relational analysis
Truth	Operationalization
Falsifiable statements	Social capital
Descriptive study	

• QUESTIONS FOR DISCUSSION

1. One version of "reality testing" in science involves comparing some observed relationship to how the results would appear if no relationship existed between variables. Look at Table 3.3 in this chapter: What would the data look like if there were no relationship between age cohort and the number of groups a person joins?

2. Do the social groups listed in this chapter reflect places where people develop "networks, norms, and social trust that facilitate coordination and cooperation for mutual benefit?" Do they jibe with your own concepts of what people do when they are part of such groups? Are unions or professional associations also groups that might build social capital?

3. Can you think of other ways of operationalizing participation in politics? Trust in government?

4. Do you think that respondents might give socially acceptable, if not entirely accurate, responses to questions about political participation? Is there any way to design a study that would avoid this problem of validity?

 ● **USEFUL WEB SITES**

National Election Study   *http://www.umich.edu/~nes/*
Look up trends in political participation and attitudes about government. The Web site includes tables that cross-tabulate survey questions by various demographic traits.

General Social Survey
http://www.icpsr.umich.edu:8080/GSS/homepage.htm
Look up responses to hundreds of questions about social and political attitudes. The Web site allows you to cross-tabulate responses to any questions in the online GSS codebook.

Bowlingalone.com   *http://www.bowlingalone.com*
Promotional material for Robert Putnam's book. Includes definitions of social capital, and free access to data used in the book.

PREVIEW OF CHAPTER FOUR

- Hypotheses
  - Values and Hypothesis Formation
  - Of Theories, Models, and Paradigms
  - Relationships in Hypotheses
- Variables
  - Operationalizing Concepts
  - Dimensions of Variables

Chapter Four

REFINEMENTS

Developing a sense for the methodology of social science resembles learning to play pool. The basic elements of each are simple—in pool, a table with pockets, some balls, and a stick; in social science, variables, measurements, and hypotheses. Up to now, we have been looking at the simple shots: a hypothesis with two fairly obvious variables and a measurement of the relations between them. In science, as in pool, the more elaborate strategies are variations on the basic technique.

A good pool player never tries a harder shot than absolutely necessary; so also with a social scientist. Likewise, professionals in both fields have had to invent techniques for minimizing error and getting around obstacles. In this chapter and the next, we will discuss the elements in a slightly different order from previous chapters—hypotheses, variables, and then measurements—and explore some refinements of each. In other words, we will illustrate some bank shots in the corner pocket.

Hypotheses

Hypotheses do not spring full-blown from the intellect unencumbered by a web of thoughts and preferences. Like any other artifact of human behavior, a hypothesis is part of a mosaic of intentions, learnings, and concerns. Social scientists have debated long and hard over how to deal with this reality. Some have preferred that the researcher do everything possible to forget values and other biases in order to concentrate on "objectively" pursuing work in the name of professional social science. Others have insisted that ignoring the origins of a hypothesis is inefficient because it leads the researcher to ignore basic factors in his or her own approach to data.

There is another whole set of questions related to how hypotheses fit with such structures of thought as theories, models, or paradigms. The formation of useful theories is, after all, the end object of the exercise. Thus, the relations between theory and research require exploration.

Finally, there is the somewhat more mundane, operational matter of the kinds of relationships that can be built into hypotheses. These three topics—the roles of values, theories, and relationships in the formation of hypotheses—will be dealt with consecutively.

Values and Hypothesis Formation

The notion of **values** is in itself peculiar. Writers have often tried to come to grips with what a value is and how one value can be separated from another. The sticky part is that values are hard to isolate. I may believe in freedom, but not freedom to the exclusion of equality, or freedom for certain kinds of behavior, such as theft. Values occur in webs of mutually modifying conditions.[1] The confused self we all experience often may be seen acting out different sets of values at different moments, with a larger pattern visible only over a substantial time period. Still there remains a kind of consistency to human character—enough so that we can and do make general estimates of the orientation to life that people have.

Social scientists generally have resolved the problem of the relation of values to research by recommending that one's value orientations be discussed in presenting a report of a project. Because values are such an intimate part of every step of forming a hypothesis, selecting measures, and evaluating conclusions, that is a fair request. However, the specification cannot be an afterthought. The role of values has to be squarely faced at the outset of inquiry. Unless that is done, you may not see what your values are doing to your research. For example, someone who is strongly religious might do research on dating habits involving questions that are premised on the immorality of premarital intercourse. The questions used might easily reflect such a bias and invite respondents to condemn a practice that they in fact approve.

Of Theories, Models, and Paradigms

The relationship of a hypothesis, or an inquiry, to theories and models of phenomena seems commonsensical but becomes steadily more complicated when authors try to set down the relationship in writing. We know what a **theory** is—a set of related propositions that attempts to explain, and sometimes to predict, a set of events. By now we also know what a hypothesis is. In a rough sense, a theory is a collection of hypotheses linked by some kind of logical framework. The term "theory" connotes a degree

---

[1]For an excellent discussion of how values relate to concepts and ideologies, see Michael Freeden, *Ideologies and Political Theory: A Conceptual Approach* (Oxford, England: Oxford University Press, 1996), Part One.

"Dynamite, Mr. Gerston! You're the first person I ever heard use 'paradigm' in real life."

of uncertainty about whether the understanding it offers is valid and correct. Theories, then, are tentative formulations. That which has been demonstrated to defy falsification usually is embodied in sets of "laws" or axioms.

Two other terms enter into the discussion. Scientists use the term **model** to convey an implication of greater order and system in a theory. Models represent simplifications of reality in a manner that allows examination of key relationships. Economists, for instance, are heavily involved in efforts to create theoretical models in which unemployment, inflation, and other major variables associated with economic performance are related mathematically.

The term **paradigm** (which comes from a Latin root meaning "pattern") refers to a larger frame of understanding, shared by a wider community of scientists, that organizes smaller-scale theories and inquiries. For generations in antiquity, astronomy was dominated by a paradigm that placed the earth at the center of the universe. Early observers of the heavens tried to explain all other stellar phenomena within that context; ultimately, of course, the paradigm collapsed with the advent of a much more powerful explanation.

There are few **laws** and **axioms** in social science, some general paradigms, a good many theories, and lately some intriguing models. For those at the beginning of social scientific investigation, theory is best conceived of as a guide to inquiry—a way of organizing and economizing insight so as to avoid the trivial and isolate the significant.

In social science there are two general modes by which theory comes into play: inductive and deductive. **Induction** refers to building theory through the accumulation and summation of a variety of inquiries. **Deduction** has to do with using the logic of a theory to generate propositions that can then be tested.

The most popular image of science has researchers collecting bits of information through a gradual process of investigation and forming them into theories. The test then becomes whether the theory explains what is known about a phenomenon. The danger in accepting the simple view of science as induction is that the categories used in constructing the inquiry may reflect an implicit theory. What is presented as induction turns out to be a hidden form of deduction. Scientific procedure is designed to reduce such biases by requiring that the propositions in a theory be put in falsifiable form: that is, that they be subject to testing through observation. As clear as that requirement would seem to be, social investigation is so value-laden and the tools for reality testing so limited that mistaken judgments can easily be made.

Deduction is becoming an increasingly common way of relating theory to research. Under pressure of attack from critics of the supposedly "objective" nature of social science, researchers are beginning to understand that deduction subtly enters into the formation of basic concepts commonly used in hypotheses. In American culture, the pervasive conditioning to a capitalist political-economic system has led many political scientists, sociologists, and economists to take our system as the norm of the good society and to cast all nonmarket patterns of behavior into such negative categories as deviant, counterproductive, underdeveloped, and so on. The connotations of these labels are, in a real sense, deduced from a larger theory that implies the naturalness or rightness of one system of political economy. Yet these labels are presented as inductively determined "scientific" designations.[2]

Proceeding from such culture-bound assumptions, it becomes easier to argue that an individual who acts on motives other than material self-interest is "poorly adjusted" or "irrational" or in need of treatment or confinement. In fact, what is labeled as irrational behavior may serve needs repressed in a capitalist society and therefore may help one adapt to a difficult environment—as, for instance, in the behavior of the poor person who buys a fancy car. Owning a car may be the one way for the person to give the appearance of success, to regard himself or herself as someone of consequence, and to attract attention from an otherwise uncaring world. That the payments deplete the food budget may strike the middle-class observer as foolish largely because middle-class observers, those with jobs at any rate, do not suffer the stress of constant rejection and personal humiliation.

Since deduction is a natural pattern of thought, it needs to be harnessed to scientific exploration. Very often deductions from theory provide the basic agenda of a field of inquiry. Established theories are guides to the solutions of many particular puzzles. The deductive route is well worth trying before starting anew in the task of explanation.

There is no need to carry this navel-gazing about induction and deduction too far. A good scientific inquiry always contains elements that make it possible for others who have differing perspectives to judge its worth. The principal reason to keep

---

[2]See Murray Edelman, *Political Languages: Words That Succeed and Policies That Fail* (New York: Academic Press, 1977).

these points in mind is to be conscious of self-delusion and of the ways others are misleading in their presentation of scientific findings.

Long before you are able to deal with the formation of theories, you will be a consumer of theory retailed by others. In utilizing research results, a precautionary question needs to be asked about the theory in terms of which the results are conceived to be meaningful. It is similar to the question about the values behind an inquiry, and it consists of understanding the theoretical perspective from which an inquiry is undertaken. Never read a social science work without paying careful attention to the introduction and preface—therein usually lies the key to the author's commitments.

At the same time, do not be afraid to play with theoretical explanation as a guide to your own efforts. Science is democratic, and anyone can take an investigative potshot at a theory or try to extend it in new ways. By becoming aware of the predominant theories in a field, you can save some of your own time by borrowing their vision to see what the possible explanations of a phenomenon are.

Relationships in Hypotheses

Independent and Dependent Variables Not all variables are equal. If social science only managed to show that prejudice is associated with ignorance, youth with rebellion, and IQ with breast-feeding, social scientists wouldn't have done as much as the culture has a right to expect. Are people prejudiced because they are ignorant, or ignorant because they wear the blinders of prejudice? Which precedes the other? We almost said, which causes the other, but did not because conclusive demonstrations of causation require elaborate procedures. The notion of independence and dependence in variables is a way of sneaking up on the question of causation without trying to go the whole distance.

An **independent variable** is one that influences another variable, called the **dependent variable.** For example, as heat increases, air can hold more water. Heat is an independent variable; the amount of water that can be suspended in the air is a dependent variable. What happens to the water depends on changes in temperature. If the air is soggy with moisture and heat goes down, water starts falling out of the air—which even social scientists refer to as rain.

In the example presented in chapter three, Putnam and others suggest that political participation **depends** on whether a person is active in voluntary social groups. **Political participation** is the dependent variable, and *membership in social groups* is the independent variable. Activity in social groups is supposed to build personal contacts and trust that give people the capacity to act politically. Thus, the hypothesis is that higher levels of activity in social groups leads to more political participation.

Reversing the relationship you are considering is a good way of seeing whether a presumed relationship of dependence makes sense. Could voting or working on political campaigns cause people to join church groups or bowling leagues? Perhaps, but you would need a convincing theory that explains why the relationship would work in that direction. The theory of social capital gives us a persuasive argument for thinking that social activity precedes political activity.

Much of the time, there's nothing very tricky about the notion of independence and dependence. If we were looking at the relationship between education and voting decisions, it's pretty clear that voting can't cause education. But there is something tricky about the fact that the relationship of independence and dependence is a figment of the researcher's imagination until demonstrated convincingly. Researchers **hypothesize** relationships of independence and dependence: they invent them, and then they try by observation and analysis to see if the relationships actually work out that way.

The question of independent and dependent variables can be more clearly understood when seen in the form social scientists are fondest of—tables. Tables are a method of presenting data, but behind a table is often a hypothesis that escapes the attention of the novice.

TABLE 4.1   POLITICAL ACTIVITY AMONG THE RICH AND POOR:
PROPORTION OF ACTIVITIES BY INCOME GROUP

	Annual Income					
	Less Than $15k	$15k to $35k	$35k to $75k	$75k to $125k	More Than $125k	Total
Dollars given to campaigns	2%	14%	29%	20%	35%	100%
Votes in elections	14	32	43	7	4	100
Contacts of officials	12	28	46	8	6	100
Protests	12	30	46	5	7	100
Hours worked on campaigns	13	30	39	8	10	100
Proportion of U.S. population	19	36	36	6	3	100

SOURCE: Sidney Verba, Kay Lehman Schlozmen, and Henry E. Brady. "The Big Tilt:
Participatory Inequality in America," *The American Prospect* (May/June 1997), available
at <http://www.prospect.org/archives/32/32verbfs.html>.

Consider Table 4.1. Which is the independent variable?
Which the dependent variable? How would you reconstruct the
hypothesis that these data support?

The two variables are income and political activity. These data
illustrate which income groups dominate certain activities. What do
these data say about the relationship between these two variables?
The answer is that the richest group, despite making up only 3 percent of the U.S. population, is proportionately much more active in
every category of political activity than less well-off groups. They
contribute 35 percent of campaign funding from individuals. The
poorest group, which makes up 19 percent of the population, contributes only 2 percent of voter-given campaign money. Income
thus affects how people in each category participate in politics.

Therefore, income is the presumed *independent* variable
and political activity is the *dependent* variable. To check on the
assignment of the labels "independent" and "dependent," reverse
the hypothesis. Could the act of voting, for example, determine
income? That doesn't make sense.

Table 4.1 illustrates the form in which tables are usually presented. The independent variable is listed across the *top* and the dependent variable down the *side*. By presenting tables in this standard fashion, researchers can locate the relationship without having to think about it. Nevertheless, it is a very good practice when looking at a table to formulate the hypotheses it is supposed to test. The author may have reversed the usual location of the independent and dependent variables for reasons of emphasis, style, or convenience.

Alternative, Antecedent, and Intervening Variables One of the central problems in developing strong hypotheses lies in understanding how variables stand in relation to each other. In hypothesizing connections between variables, you need to be aware of variables other than the ones you have selected that may be involved in producing changes in a relationship. Social scientists commonly refer to *alternative, antecedent,* and *intervening variables.*

All three terms have commonsense meanings. An **alternative variable** is an additional independent variable that influences changes in the dependent variable. An antecedent is something that comes before. For example, the antecedent of birth is conception. To intervene means to come between. We will illustrate each of these concepts more precisely.

If one considers the variables that influence who contributes to political campaigns, several appear: gender, race, occupation, partisanship, attitudes about government, and other factors might matter. These are alternative variables. Establishing the link between income and contributing to campaigns (see Table 4.1) is useful nonetheless, though a complete account of why people do or do not contribute would have to include the influence of all the significant alternative variables. Income clearly does influence contributing, but gender and other variables intervene. If important variables are left out, the results may be meaningless or—as social scientists like to say—*spurious.* We shall return to the issue of spuriousness in the next chapter.

A classic illustration of an **antecedent variable** comes from the history of research on voting behavior. It became obvious from early surveys that more highly educated people tend to vote

Republican. From that relationship, it could be implied that well-educated people are politically conservative. However, it turns out that a powerful antecedent variable influences both the *level of education* and *voting behavior: parental wealth.* In fact, those who are highly educated tend to come from wealthier families, and wealthier families are more likely to vote Republican. What was being measured in the correlation of *education* with *voting behavior* was really the prior influence of *parental wealth* on the political preferences of their children.

As for **intervening variables,** suppose you are told that Hollygood Bread has fewer calories per slice than six other brands. The advertising leads you to assume that the independent variable is Hollygood's special formula for low-calorie dough. But you come to find out that the real reason for the difference is that the Hollygood company slices its bread thinner than the others. The dough actually has about as many calories as Sunshaft Bread or even Wondergoo. The thinness of the slice is the intervening variable between quality of dough and calories per slice.

To use a more elegant example, consider the relationship between education and social status. These two variables are positively associated; however, everyone knows of people who have modest educations but high social status. The reason might be that another variable enters the picture: occupational success.

To see how occupational success intervenes between education and status, think of the people you know who are poorly educated but who enjoy average status by virtue of their success at their job (group A). Now think of those who are well educated, successful, and high in status (group B). Think of yet a third group who are well educated but who have had lousy luck in the job market and have middling status by conventional standards (group C).

If you worked only with the relationship between education and status or that between occupation and status, rather than with all three variables, you would miss the point of the relationship between either pair. Group A would have you thinking that there is little connection between education and status, yet group B would make it appear that status and education go together like peanut butter and jelly. Meanwhile group C, just as educated as group B, has only average status. The same confusion would result from considering only the relationship between occupational success and status.

In general, well-educated people (group B) have higher status than poorly educated people (group A). Thus, it is demonstrable that education contributes to success. However, occupational success intervenes between education and conventional social status.

The way to avoid getting trapped by alternative, antecedent, and intervening variables is to do some thinking before formulating a hypothesis. Take the dependent variable and ask yourself what all the possible independent variables might be. If you want to explain why some people are fatalistic, think of all the variables that could influence such a state of mind. Possibilities might include the nature of their work, money troubles, unrequited love, background characteristics, the weather, or peer-group influences. In fact, most social phenomena—perhaps *all* social phenomena—are influenced by several variables. The point of worrying about alternative, antecedent, and intervening variables is not so much to discourage investigation of what interests you as to put it into perspective so that you do not confuse association with causation.

As another example, consider the argument frequently heard during election campaigns over the effect of state taxes on the employment rate. Critics of the cost of government are heard to argue that lowering taxes and spending will stimulate the state's economy by attracting businesses that don't like to pay taxes, thus adding new jobs and reducing unemployment. In Figure 4.1, we have indicated some of the antecedent, intervening, and alternative variables that might have an impact on a state's unemployment rate.

A careful sorting out reveals that many independent variables are involved, any one of which is likely to be more significant than the one hypothesized: state taxing and spending policies. In fact, the relationships among these variables is fairly complex. State political institutions such as direct democracy can cause lower taxes and spending through initiatives and referenda. However,

FIGURE 4.1   INDEPENDENT VARIABLES AFFECTING UNEMPLOYMENT

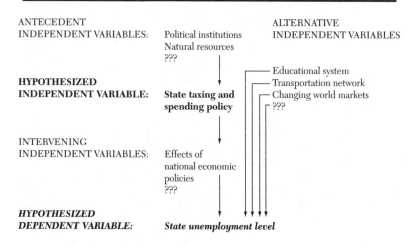

higher state taxes, insofar as they finance the educational system, may be the key to improving employment in a state.[3]

Once you recognize the variables that have a significant influence on a dependent variable, there are ways of separating out the influence of one variable from another. The simplest technique is to "control" for one variable by holding it constant, while two others are tested for their relationship to each other. In the example of the connections between parental wealth, education, and voting behavior, one could select a sample of respondents with various levels of education from families of different wealth characteristics. If it turns out that highly educated children of wealthy families are predominantly Republicans, and that highly educated children of poorer families are predominantly Democrats, you know that education is far less powerful than family wealth in shaping voting behavior. Tables 4.2 and 4.3 illustrate this result.

---

[3]See, for example, Bryan D. Jones, "Public Policies and Economic Growth in the American States," *Journal of Politics* 52 (1990): 219–234. Jones finds that the overall size of the public sector is not associated with economic decline and that spending on education, highways, police, and fire protection is associated with employment gains and economic growth.

TABLE 4.2   EDUCATION AND PARTY IDENTIFICATION

Party Identification	Low Education	High Education	Total
Democrat	150	50	200
Republican	50	150	200
Total	200	200	400

SOURCE: Simulated.

TABLE 4.3   EDUCATION AND PARTY IDENTIFICATION,
CONTROLLING FOR WEALTH

	From Poor Families			From Wealthy Families		
Party Identification	Low Education	High Education	Total	Low Education	High Education	Total
Democrat	100	45	145	50	5	55
Republican	5	10	15	45	140	185
Subtotal			160			240

SOURCE: Simulated.

As your methodological experience and sophistication increase, you will discover a host of techniques by which these connections can be sorted out. The first step in approaching the problem of sorting out variables is to understand the different levels of relationships that are built into hypotheses.

Levels of Relationships in Hypotheses

The most distinctive characteristic of a hypothesis as opposed to most ordinary sentences is the care with which each term is specified. We have seen that the selection of variables is a serious task in itself; so also with the relationships that are specified between variables. In order to stretch your imagination a little, it is worth considering systematically the possible relationships that can be expressed between two or more variables. They compose a spectrum, and we will discuss briefly each of the relationships presented in Table 4.4.

TABLE 4.4   TYPES OF RELATIONSHIPS BETWEEN VARIABLES

Relationship	Meaning
Null	No relationship is presumed to exist.
Inferential/Correlative	A relationship is presumed, but it is a relationship that deals with degrees of influence of one variable on another.
Direct/Inverse	Specific correlative relationship is presumed in which one variable has a predictable association with another—either one variable increases as the other increases (direct) or one increases while the other decreases (inverse).
Causal	Changes in one variable are presumed to result from variations in another.

The first relationship, the **null hypothesis,** is a rather ingenious creation. Remember that hypotheses are imagined relationships that are then put to the test. There is something to be said for positing no relationship and then testing to see if the null hypothesis can be disproved, that is, if it can be demonstrated that some relationship does indeed exist.

The utility of the null hypothesis is that the case is not prejudged—you are not caught defending a relationship specified beforehand. In addition to withholding commitment to a specific relationship, you are also leaving open the possibility that one of the more substantial relationships may characterize the connection between the variables. It may be that there is an **inferential** or a **correlative relationship** that will emerge from the reality test. There may even be a **direct** or an **inverse relationship,** but those possibilities are left to emerge from the test itself.

The null hypothesis is admirably suited to a cautious strategy of social investigation. A null hypothesis can be disproven simply by demonstrating that there is *any* sort of association between two variables. Causation requires an enormous burden of proof and is at the opposite end of the relationship spectrum from the null hypothesis.

Inferential and correlative relationships can be tested as a preliminary to moving in on **causal relationships.** The lesser relationships, interesting in themselves, are also screening devices. If, in the example of the relationship between education and voter assessments of candidates, a correlation that is statistically significant can be demonstrated, then there is some reason to press ahead with the work of separating out extraneous sources of error that may be responsible for the correlation. That done, the alternative sources of causation may be tested to see if a causal hypothesis might be justified.

Several things need to be understood about the relationship of causation. First, it is probably the end object of social science to decide what causes what. Therefore, there is tremendous interest in establishing causality. Second, it is the most difficult relationship to deal with because it demands the highest burden of proof. To prove that A causes B, you need to demonstrate that:

1. A *happens before* B. Obvious, isn't it?
2. *The occurrence of A is connected with the occurrence of B.* This is obvious as well, but the connections of events are not always simple to discover. Some historians, for example, find a consistent link between the diets of reformers in the Middle Ages and the elaborateness of their visions. Joan of Arc, it is claimed, ate the wrong things, fouled up her digestive system, and so became a visionary and temporary heroine!
3. A *causes B; there isn't some other variable (C) that eliminates the variation in B associated with A.* This is where the going gets tough. It is always hard to eliminate all the possible influences, save one, in a situation. The time-honored technique in experimental social science is to select two groups of subjects, duplicate as closely as possible everything in the environments of the two groups, and introduce the suspected causal variable to one group (the experimental group) and not to the other (the control group).

A classic example of the problems that arise in using the experimental-control group technique is the "Hawthorne" experiments, wherein one group of workers, the experimental group, was placed in a more pleasing physical environment for their assembly-line work. This experimental group consistently outproduced the control group, those working in the usual factory conditions. The trouble is that the increased productivity was later discovered to be mostly the effect of another variable—the special attention given the experimental group by the managers and experimenters themselves—rather than the physical surroundings. The experimenter had unknowingly introduced uncontrolled psychological factors: the two groups were differentiated by more than physical decor, thus violating the experimental-control group procedure and invalidating the results.

Most social scientists view the understanding of causation as the culmination of a long process of hypothesis formation and testing. The usual technique is to begin with a series of experiments to isolate the one variable that has the most obvious connection to the caused event. By this means, suspected sources of causation can be identified. The remaining logical steps usually demand a very high order of experimental elaboration. Consequently, beginners in the field are better off staying with relationships that can be more easily managed.

Because social science involves issues of great personal importance, it is hard to cultivate the habit of caution in hypothesis formation. Most beginners overstate their hypotheses, which leads them into measurement difficulties and the disappointments of an overworked conclusion. In trying to decide how strong a relationship to test for, give some thought to the measurements available as well as to the data resources within reach. A completely reported research experiment always contains the researcher's speculations about the larger ramifications of the results. But these are more palatable if the study itself observes sensible limits of hypothesis statement and measurement technique.

Establishing the logical relationships between variables in a hypothesis is, of course, a separate matter from testing to see if those relationships hold up. To see if a hypothesized relationship actually is borne out by observation, we need to move to the techniques of operationalization and measurement.

Variables

Operationalizing Concepts

Early in our discussion of social scientific concepts, we saw how language begins with the problem of assigning names to different phenomena. Social scientific language consists of agreements between people that a given behavior is properly referred to by a given name. To operationalize a variable means essentially to fit the name used for a behavior to some specific way of observing and measuring that behavior. Variable operationalizing, in a way, reverses the process by which language is formed: Start with the name of the phenomenon that interests you, and work backward to find ways of tying that name to the specific behavior to which it refers.

The word *operationalization* makes the process discussed here sound special and expert, when in fact it is commonplace in everyday life. Late one evening, one of the authors of this book heard an argument in a saloon over which people are better, Kentuckians or West Virginians. The "discussion" revolved around such items as the observation that one person's cousin's uncle's father-in-law was from Kentucky and he was no damn good. However, by comparison, it seems that the other person's former boss married a woman whose nephew was from West Virginia and he was born to be hanged! After several volleys of this sort, it became clear that the variable, the quality of *Kentuckians* and *West Virginians,* had been operationalized in terms of the affinity for criminal behavior of people living in those states.

As any science develops, the number of variable names that refer to carefully specified objects, events, or behaviors increases. There are now in the social sciences whole catalogues of variables operationalized in terms of specific behaviors and possible measurements.[4]

---

[4]See John Robinson, Phillip Shaver and Lawrence Wrightsman, *Measures of Political Attitudes* (San Diego, Calif.: Academic Press, 1999).

With a little luck, the variables that interest you have already been operationalized in a variety of ways. Even so, you need to know a number of techniques for operationalization in order to gain analytical flexibility and to be critical of what other people have done. In addition, you need to learn how to get around problems that arise when variables require forms of measurement that are outside your resources. There are two ways of dealing with a variable that, for some reason, is not amenable to operationalization: **substitution** and **division.**

Suppose your hypothesis is this: *The more educated people are, the more likely they are to be socialists.* Education isn't hard to operationalize: the number of years spent in school tells you about exposure to formal education.

Whether people are socialists, and if so, how socialistic they are, is quite another matter. The ideology called socialism brings together a complex of theories, versions of history, plans for action, and standards of good and bad. This bundle of things becomes all the harder to understand when it is realized that scholars of the subject have trouble agreeing on just what socialism means. Added to the difficulty of isolating a standard definition of socialism is the problem of dealing with unshared interpretations of the word on the part of the researcher, who is presumably trained in the formal ideological concept, and the sample survey respondent, who may think socialists are people who favor fluoridated water.

So it won't do to ask people, "Are you a socialist and, if so, how much of a socialist?" The answers to that question would generate some interesting data on self-perception, but the question would be too sloppy as a means of relating the respondents' attitudes to something as elaborate as socialist philosophy. *Substituting* for the variable *socialism* might solve some of those problems. Another variable could be found that pins down the attitudes involved more directly and deals with them in concrete terms. How about: *The more educated people become, the more they favor worker participation in management.*

The advantage here is that questions can be asked on a matter most people have an opinion about, and in terms that they can relate to. It does provide information relevant to the general hypothesis by picking up on an important element of socialist ideology even though it is a substitution.

Division is another way of dealing with a difficult variable. Behavior is very seldom simple; it occurs in the context of related actions, attitudes, and dispositions. Often the variables social scientists deal with can be seen as combinations of behavioral ingredients. The variable *alienation*, for example, may be divided into four specific characteristics that are tied to the way people are thought to feel when they are alienated: normless, powerless, meaningless, and helpless. Attitude scales have been developed to try to measure each of those attitude ingredients of alienation. By combining measures of all four attitudes or feelings, you will have data that could respectably be said to have something to do with alienation.

Dimensions of Variables

Variables often have different **dimensions.** A psychologist measuring personality might come up with a classification of introverted and extroverted personalities. He or she might also come up with a characterization of aggressivity–passivity on a scale from 1 to 10. These represent different dimensions of one variable: *personality.*

Public opinion usually is analyzed in terms of a variety of dimensions:

Direction: The *for*-ness or *against*-ness of the opinion
Location: Where on the scale from *for* to *against* is the opinion found?
Intensity: How strongly or weakly held is the opinion?
Stability: How changeable is it?
Latency: How close to the surface of the opinion structures is it?
Salience: How important is that opinion in relation to others the person holds?[5]

---

[5]Adapted from Bradlee Karan, "Pubic Opinion and the New Ohio Criminal Code," The College of Wooster Symposium on Public Opinion and the New Ohio Criminal Code,

All these dimensions contain different measurement possibilities and a variety of techniques are available to handle them. The *direction* of opinion requires only a specification that tells whether the opinion is on the "yes" side or the "no" side. *Salience,* on the other hand, allows an ordering of opinions from no salience to very great salience. *Intensity* of opinion suggests the possibility of scaling.

Before doing much work on a variable, think over which dimension you are looking at and what the other possible dimensions might be. Select those dimensions that are most promising in getting to the core of the variable. By looking at alternative dimensions, you can make choices as to which dimensions get to the crux of the variable and which dimensions can be measured by the means available to you. At the same time, understanding the different dimensions of a variable provides perspective on what has or has not yet been done to understand the variable.

One of the most persistent myths about science is that it can be entirely equated with measurement. As this chapter has tried to make clear, the real creativity in science goes into the operationalization of variables and the design of hypotheses. These very often require genuine creativity. Although measurement occasionally approaches an art form, it is more typically a matter of technique and the systematic application of mathematical concepts. As we shall see in the next chapter, measurement has its own logic and clever devices.

July 9–30, 1973, pp. 6–8 and Vladimir Orlando Key Jr., *Public Opinion and American Democracy* (New York: Knopf, 1961), pp. 11–18.

Key discusses variables in terms of their *properties* rather than their *dimensions.* With respect to public opinion, be uses the term "dimensions" where we have used "location," In recent usage, the term "properties" has become a general name for all the characteristics of a variable: its measurements as well as its various substantive components, or dimensions, which have acquired the more specific meaning to which we refer.

• CONCEPTS INTRODUCED

Values	Antecedent variable
Theory	Intervening variable
Models	Null hypothesis
Paradigms	Inferential relationship
Laws	Correlative relationship
Axioms	Direct relationship
Induction	Inverse relationship
Deduction	Causal relationship
Independent variable	Variable substitution
Dependent variable	Variable division
Alternative variable	Dimensions of variables

• QUESTIONS FOR DISCUSSION

NOTE: Examine the data represented in Table 4.2 and Table 4.3. In this example, Table 4.2 is said to examine the relationship between education and party identification. In Table 4.3, party identification for people from both poor and wealthy families is examined. Table 4.3 introduces a control for family wealth, since party identification might also be associated with family wealth.

1. How does the original pattern seen in Table 4.2 change when we examine the two groups in Table 4.3?

2. Is the relationship between party identification and education affected by income?

3. What do the results in Table 4.3 indicate about the relationship between education and party identification?

4. Can you think of any logical explanation for the patterns displayed in the tables? What variable(s) is/are dependent? What variable(s) is/are independent? Why?

5. Looking at the variables in the regression analysis in the Brockington et al. article (Appendix B), does it make sense to think that levels of minority representation depend upon election rules and the size of a community's minority population? Could the causal process work in some other direction?

PREVIEW OF CHAPTER FIVE

- Measuring Variables: Levels of Measurement
- Measuring the Significance and Representativeness of Data:
  Probability, Sampling, and Problems in Polling
- Measuring Relationships between Variables:
  Association and Correlation
- Association
  - Measures of Association and Correlation
  - Regression Analysis
  - Why Multiple Regression? Control and Spuriousness
  - Probit and Logit Analysis
- Computers and Statistics

Chapter Five

MEASURING VARIABLES AND RELATIONSHIPS

"He that makes Coates for the Moone, had need take measure every noone."

–NATHANIEL WARD

Scientists basically measure three things: *variables, the chances that data about variables are meaningful*, and *relationships between variables*. Each of these measurement tasks has distinctive approaches and statistical devices. As we look at ideas used in accomplishing these tasks, remember that measurement almost always looks more precise than it really is.

The term *measurement* will be used rather broadly in this chapter. For the first topic, the measurement of variance, we will examine the kinds of measurement suited to different types of variables. Next, we will look at techniques for describing the significance and representativeness of data obtained through scientific procedures. There are techniques for making fairly precise judgments about the chances that a set of data may be simply the result of a freakish sample rather than a meaningful measurement. In this connection, we show how sample surveys are constructed and discuss some common polling errors. Then, we present some ideas about measuring relationships *between* variables. The objective is to grasp the basic tools for reducing data about two or more related variables into a statistic that characterizes the relationship between them.

Conventionally, *measurement* as a term applies only to the first of these topics. The second concerns the problem of the significance and representativeness of data and uses probability, which isn't, in the narrowest sense, a form of measurement. The third is often seen as a question of characterizing the association between things rather than of measurement strictly speaking. Yet all three topics have to do with establishing quantities of something: variance, significance, and association. Consequently, all three topics have been fitted under the general rubric of measurement.

Measuring Variables: Levels of Measurement

Measurement is a deceptive subject. At first, it seems simple—measurement answers the question, "How much?" This appears easy enough to answer when talking about length or weight, but not so easy when considering such common fodder for social science as information levels, personal characteristics, feelings, and attitudes. The reason for the difficulty resides not so much in the matter of counting up units of things as in the nature of the things being counted.

In measuring variables, for example, three considerations determine what level of measurement can be attempted and, therefore, what sort of hypothetical relationships can be formulated using the variable:

1. The *properties* or characteristics of the variable
2. The measurement *technique* appropriate to these properties

3. The *levels* of measurement that are possible in view of the variable's properties and available techniques

Consider, for example, a variable such as marital status. The variable refers to a classification according to a legal definition: single (with the subdivisions of unmarried, divorced, or widowed) or married (with perhaps the subdivision of monogamous or polygamous). In "measuring" someone's marital status, the property of the variable dictates that you can't do more than categorize—it's not possible to say that someone is very much married or very little married. In the eyes of the law, you either are or are not married. Given such a *property*, the variable *marital status* doesn't call for very fancy measurement *technique*.

The variable *intelligence* poses different possibilities for measurement. The **properties** of the variable do not limit consideration to mere classification: the variable has properties that imply larger and smaller amounts. This is where *technique* comes in. People have puzzled for centuries over how to measure intelligence. Efforts have included tests such as the sense to come in out of the rain—in which case intelligence can be measured in two categories: those who do, and those who don't, have the sense to come in out of the rain. Research marches on, however, and we have the IQ test. The IQ test gives us a reading on how well people can answer certain kinds of questions that are thought to have something to do with intelligence. This advance in technique permits fairly detailed gradations between the low and high ends of a scale associated with intelligence.

Measurement comprises an area of research all by itself. Researchers keep trying to develop measurement techniques that can explore all the properties of important variables. In order to systematize our understanding of various kinds of possible measurements, scientists have come up with a classification of four levels of measurement:

1. Normal
2. Ordinal
3. Interval
4. Ratio

In Figure 5.1 the characteristics of these levels are explored. The **nominal** level doesn't quite seem like measurement; it refers to classifications of things. Take ethnicity for an example. If Sinnikka is a Finn and Igor is a Russian, we have said something about the properties of each person in relation to a variable called *ethnicity*. That's measurement, but not very fancy measurement. We can't rate Finns above Russians (except according to some other variable, such as fondness for pickled herring—and even then, it would be close). Therefore classification, or nominal measurement, is all that the properties of *ethnicity* as a variable allow.[1] Nominal measurement, low grade as it is, pops up frequently in social science, as the examples listed in the figure indicate: race, region, sex, occupation, and so on.

If the properties of the variable allow ordering as well as classification, the **ordinal** level of measurement can be attempted, provided the techniques are available. At this level, we can think in terms of a continuum—that is, an array that indicates variation, as opposed to simple classification. Class is one illustration, and socioeconomic standing is another. We can say that Alphonse is upper class, while Mack is lower class. These are classifications, but they are arranged in such a way as to link them on a continuum from lower to higher. Similarly with formal education: Angelina has a Ph.D., Mary a high school education, and Jane a grade school certificate. However, a Ph.D. isn't the same "distance" from a college degree as a high school diploma is from a grade school certificate. Ordering, yes; standard distance, no. The specification of distance—or, more generally, the amount of variation between cases—is an important step up in the realm of measurement. Distance affords a decided increase in the sophistication with which a variable can be measured and related to other variables.

---

[1]We could, *within* each ethic group, identify on the basis of parentage what proportion of a person's heritage belongs to an ethnic grouping, but the notion of ethnicity itself is classificatory.

FIGURE 5.1 LEVELS OF MEASUREMENT

Level	Variable Properties Allow You To:	Illustration	Examples
1. Nominal	Classify	*Russian:* Igor *Finnish:* Sinnikka *Norwegian:* Olaf	Ethnicity, race, region, sex, marital status, occupation, group affiliation
2. Ordinal	Classify Order	Lower Class — Lower Middle Class — Middle Class — Upper Middle Class — Upper Class	Class, socioeconomic standing, formal education
3. Interval	Classify Order Set standard units of distance	1000 B.C. — 500 B.C. — 0 — 500 A.D. — 1000 A.D. — 1500 A.D. — 2000 A.D. — 2500 A.D. — 3000 A.D.; ZERO (Arbitrary)	Biblical time, Fahrenheit temperature
4. Ratio	Classify Order Set standard units of distance Locate absolute zero	0 — $2,000 — $4,000 — $6,000 — $8,000 — $10,000 — $12,000 — $14,000 — $16,000; ZERO (True)	Income, age, wealth, distance

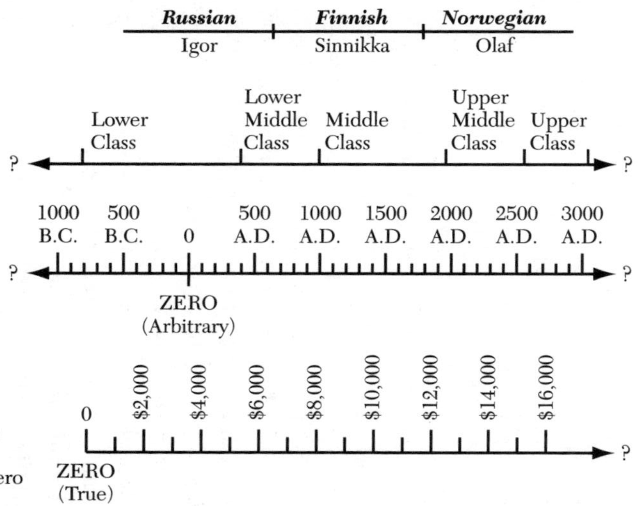

97

If standard distance can be achieved, the next level of measurement enters the picture: **interval** measurement. Here, units can be identified that indicate how far each case is from each other case. That's reasonable, but there remains one of those technicalities that causes confusion of the mind. It has to do with absolute zero on a scale of measurement.

Interval measures do not have a **true zero.** What is a true zero? And what good is it? In the example of biblical time, the year 'zero' doesn't mean that nothing happened before then. We don't really know where true zero is in history. Zero was established in relationship to the life of Christ for religious reasons and serves as a convenient reference point for counting forward and backward. The same is true of Fahrenheit temperature. You know that 0 degrees Fahrenheit doesn't represent a true zero because –23 degrees is a lot colder than 0 degrees.

A **ratio** scale does have a true zero. A ratio scale such as distance is different from an interval scale because, for example, in a ratio scale zero inches means just that—no distance at all. There can't be less than zero distance, or less than zero weight, or less than zero bananas. That tells you the formal difference between a true zero and an **arbitrary zero,** or one that is made up for the sake of convenience.

But what good is a true zero? The answer has to do with what can be said in comparing observations on a ratio or an interval scale. If Hardy weighs 200 pounds and Laurel weighs 100 pounds (ratio scale), we can see that Hardy is twice as heavy as Laurel. But if the temperature is 50 degrees on Monday and 25 degrees on Wednesday (interval scale), can we really say that it was twice as hot on Monday as on Wednesday? You can try to get away with it, but you really shouldn't, because a comparison of that kind requires a *true zero.* You need to know what the total absence of heat is when making out that one day was twice as hot as another. Without a beginning point, *distances* can be established, but not *ratios.*

The reason for knowing these distinctions has to do with the kind of relationships that can be established statistically within and between variables. The job is to avoid comparison of apples and oranges. Statistics enter this text only in the form of ideas behind numbers—the arithmetic and the finer points of various statistical operations are left to more technical writings. Here we will content ourselves with a simple point (simple as statistics go). Roughly speaking:

> *Nominal* measurement allows statistics having to do with frequency of cases in each classification (e.g., ethnicity: 10 Finns, 3 Russians).
>
> *Ordinal* measurement allows statistics that describe the way the cases are ordered with respect to a variable (e.g., education: grade school, high school, college).
>
> *Interval* measurement permits comparisons of quantitative differences among cases on a scale (e.g., time: 1950, 1990).
>
> *Ratio* measurement permits comparisons of absolute distances between cases (e.g., money: $10, $20).[2]

Because these levels of measurement are key to how relations between variables can be approached, it is essential to figure out the appropriate level of measurement for each variable before proceeding with research. We will see the significance of levels of measurement spelled out in more detail as we turn to the problem of measuring variable *relationships* in the form of correlations.

---

[2]From Sidney Siegel, *Nonparametric Statistics for the Social Sciences* (New York: McGraw-Hill, 1956), p. 30. See also Chava Frankfort-Nachmias and David Nachmias, *Research Methods in the Social Sciences*, 6th ed. (New York: St. Martin's: 2000), Chapter 7.

For those who are familiar with statistics, the following is a *partial* list of examples of statistics appropriate for each level:

Nominal: mode, frequency, contingency table

Ordinal: median, percentile, Spearman's *rho*, Kendall's *tau*, Goodnam-Kruskal's *gamma*

Interval: mean, standard deviation, Pearson's product moment correlation, multiple correlation

Ratio: geometric mean, coefficient of variation, OLS regression

*Measuring the Significance and
Representativeness of Data: Probability,
Sampling, and Problems in Polling*

We now turn to these topics that fit together not so much because of their general connection with measurement, but because they all relate to understanding the strengths and weaknesses of data that are to be analyzed. The topics are probability, sampling, and problems in polling. Polling provides a useful arena for examining sampling and probability, but these topics also have much wider applications in social science.

To get hold of the statistical tools basic to scientific research, we need to become familiar with a new concept: **probability.** Probability occupies a far more important place in social science than the amount of space devoted to it in this book would suggest. Probability constitutes nothing less than a fundamental of the scientific perspective. To understand why is to come to grips with some particularly ornery habits of the human mind.

Probability refers to the likelihood or chance of something occurring. We compute probabilities about the chances of passing a course, the prospects for a date, the odds of a team winning a game. That *Roget's Thesaurus* lists so many alternatives for the word *probability*—luck, hazard, fortuity, fate, contingency, chance, and others—indicates the importance of the concept in our language.

We began by saying that science becomes useful to human beings as a way of coping with the uncertainties of life. By forcing ideas and notions out of the head and into the arena of empirical observation and by testing them, we gain knowledge about the world. The scientific establishment is built on the power provided by the effort to escape the insecurity of uncertainty about our surroundings. However, it is characteristic of scientific knowledge that it is rarely cast in stone. Often explicitly and always implicitly, scientific generalizations are probabilistic.

Science is the refinement of chance far more often than the discovery of certainty. Indeed, social scientists often discuss their findings in a language that expresses the possibility of being wrong. We worry about the odds that a set of results reflects an inaccurate sample, or that another researcher would find different results from ours. Formally, we rarely speak of social science as conclusively *proving* anything.[3] Rather, we speak of the *probability* that a hypothesis is supported by the available evidence.

As an illustration of the way probability is built into social science, we shall consider two special applications of probability statistics: determining the statistical significance of the array of data, and constructing representative samples of larger populations. Yet the objective is the same in both: trying to specify the odds that a display of data reveals something more than a chance relationship between variables. If the information is based on a faulty sample or if it represents merely a freak combination of cases, then the results can't be said to tell us anything conclusive about the relationship between the variables. It is important to know that, and probability statistics provide some tools.

The first usage of probability concerns the representativeness of a sample drawn from a larger population. Given the size and characteristics of a sample, what is the probability that we can *infer* from a sample some specific characteristics of a population? This form of probability underlies public-opinion polling. Pollsters often try to estimate the percentage of the public that intends to vote for a specific candidate. In attempting to characterize the behavior of a huge group of people, it is nearly always impossible to survey everyone. Selecting the smallest, most representative possible sample is the key to efficiency in polling. Probability statistics are used to estimate the chances that a sample is representative.

---

[3]An influential critique of positivism from within the philosophy of science can be found in W. V. O. Quine, "The Two Dogmas of Empiricism," *From a Logical Point of View*, ed. W. V. O. Quine (New York: Harper & Row, 1961). See also Alexander Rosenberg, *The Structure of Biological Science* (Cambridge, England: Cambridge University Press, 1985).

The second application of probability involves estimating the likelihood of a set of observations occurring by chance. If there is only one chance in a hundred that the results we are seeing would have occurred randomly, then the pattern is quite significant. A pattern of data linking two variables (say, income and education) that has a chance of occurring randomly one time in a hundred tells us something useful. Without probing the mathematics, we would refer to this result as *significant at the .01 level.* Significance statistics are derived by combining the number of observations in the sample, the amount of variation in the variables, and the magnitude of the observed relationship. The most likely random distribution of results would show the same number of cases in each cell of a table; the least likely would have all the cases in one cell.

Establishing the **level of significance** of the results constitutes an important test of the hypothesis. Results demonstrating that all upper-income people are highly educated, and that all lower-income people are poorly educated, are most unlikely to occur by chance. The independent variable has a very strong impact on the dependent variable. There is very likely a correlation between income and education in the population. Significance tests tell us, under certain conditions, the probability that our hypothesis is right (or wrong).

In its most basic form, significance tells us "whether or not a certain relationship . . . is worth further thought—whether it might repay additional research effort."[4] Some social scientists will deal only with data significant at the .01 level, whereas others accept .05 as the cutoff—meaning that there are five chances (as opposed to one chance) out of 100 of the observed relationship occurring by chance. The significance level is commonly noted as part of a research report, which helps in evaluating results.

The two uses of probability we have been discussing are related: the first deals with whether the sample is representative,

---

[4]For a lucid and accessible discussion of significance testing, see Lawrence Mohr, *Understanding Significance Tests,* Sage University Paper Series on Quantitative Applications in the Social Sciences, no. 73 (Beverly Hills, Calif.: Sage Publications, 1990).

and the second concerns the chances that the results are meaningful. Loosely stated, the questions become:

Is the sample representative? [inference]
Is the pattern of results likely to have occurred by chance? [significance]

A representative sample provides a sound basis for inferring the level of support for a hypothesis, especially if the pattern of observations is statistically significant. A poor sample, however, will make for poor inferences whether or not the pattern of data is significant. A sample drawn according to probability theory is known, not surprisingly, as a **probability sample.**

There are two general techniques used in sampling: stratification and random sampling. **Stratification** involves trying to reproduce a large population by representing important characteristics proportionately in the sample. If we tried to determine a community's attitude toward drinking by interviewing a sample of customers at a local saloon, that sample would overrepresent one segment of the public in terms of a characteristic vital to the issue under consideration. Teetotalers don't hang out in saloons. Therefore, we would have to select the sample in such a way that teetotalers have a chance of being included.

If the stratification method were used to select a sample for determining voting behavior in an election, we would try to have a sample that reflected proportionately the larger population—at least in terms of such significant independent variables as class, region, and education. However, the stratification (proportionate sampling of certain characteristics of voters) must be limited to a relatively small number of characteristics. Otherwise, in order to fill out the sample with representatives of all the variables in the proper proportion, we might wind up spending valuable resources trying to find people with highly unlikely combinations of characteristics.

Random sampling depends on selecting at random a sufficient sample of the population such that there is a high probability of reproducing the essential characteristics of the total population. The likelihood of representativeness increases in predictable fashion as the size of the sample grows. For example, if we interview five randomly selected people out of a national population of 210 million, the chances are not so good that they are truly representative—there would be a very high margin of error. With each increase in the size of the sample, provided the people are selected randomly, the margin of error decreases.

For any size population, it is possible to determine mathematically the probability that a given sample size will generate a specifiable margin of error. The margin of error drops drastically with the increasing size of the sample, up to a point at which further increases in sample size reduce the margin of error very little. It is this point that indicates the most economical sample size. By doubling or tripling the sample size beyond this point, or even multiplying it by 10, relatively little reduction of error can be achieved.

One major problem with random sampling is that in order to interview all of those who are selected, the interviewers have to disperse their efforts and seek out respondents in all corners of the total population. Most scientific sampling uses both stratification and randomization. For example, in a national sample, one might select representative urban areas and representative rural areas (a form of stratification) and then draw a random sample within those target areas.

Telephone sampling, although it contains a bias against those who have no phones, has become an increasingly popular technique now that computers make it possible to do random digit dialing within specific telephone exchanges. Evolutions in communications technology are introducing new biases to phone sampling, however. Pagers, beepers, and answering machines are hooked up on many telephone exchanges. Annoyance with heavy telemarketing efforts might be boosting refusal rates for survey researchers. Good phone samples may still be drawn, but costs are increasing as researchers act to minimize these new biases. The Internet creates new possibilities for establishing panels of respondents who can be polled on important questions.

For their surveys of American opinion, major academic, commercial, and media polls (Pew Research, Gallup, Harris, CNN/*USA Today*, CBS/*New York Times*, ABC News/*Washington Post*, NBC/*Wall Street Journal*) use a stratified random sample so as to eliminate, among other problems, the inconvenience of interviewing a randomly selected sheepherder in a remote section of Nevada. The sample size is typically about 1,500 persons. At this size, the margin of error is about 3 percent at the .05 level of significance. What this means is that 95 samples out of 100 should produce a measure of the opinions of the actual population, within a range of plus or minus 3 percent. So if 49 percent of the actual population plan to vote Democrat, then 95 out of 100 samples would produce estimates ranging between 46 and 52 percent.[5]

The major media firms have had fairly impressive record of achievement in using samples of this kind to predict presidential elections, in part because they have been lucky in not drawing a "way-out" sample, one of the five in a hundred, and in part because they do stratify their samples somewhat to avoid the weird sample that might occur if simple random sampling were used. This does not mean their predictions are perfect. CBS/*New York Times* polls taken immediately prior to the 1996 election overestimated Clinton's victory margin by as much as 10 percent. *The Times* concluded that its sample of the 'probable electorate' was not appropriate.[6]

Prediction is also difficult if you are trying to use a sample to represent real values that are nearly indistinguishable from each other. On election night in 2000, data from exit polls used by the major networks twice led them to predict the wrong outcome in Florida. This led them to declare that Gore, rather than Bush, was elected president. One problem in Florida was that the election there was so close—essentially a 49 percent to 49 percent

[5] We thank Albert Klumpp for this example.
[6] See Michael R. Kagay, "Experts See a Need for Redefining Election Polls," *New York Times* (December 15, 1996), p. A18.

tie.[7] For the networks to call Florida in favor of Gore, their polling data must have shown that he had a lead of *at least* 1 to 2 percent to be confident their prediction was beyond the margin for error.[8]

The 2000 Florida exit polls failed by showing, *with confidence,* that Gore received more votes that Bush. This does not mean that the prediction about who won was totally wrong. Exit polls measure who voters *thought* they voted for on election day. A plurality of Florida voters probably did try to vote for Gore on election day—but voter error, equipment failure, and overseas ballots that were counted illegally *after* the election muddled the final count and probably cost Gore the presidency.[9] Even with all these things accounted for, the polls overestimated the proportion of voters who believed they had voted for Gore. The true margin between Gore and Bush was still less than .05 percent. A perfectly representative sample should have shown this and lead the networks to realize it was too close to call.

Another way of understanding sampling is to consider how poor samples lead to faulty conclusions. Bad samples have led to some major mistakes in forecasting presidential elections. A now-defunct publication, the *Literary Digest,* made itself famous by surveying millions of voters per election and forecasting (accurately) the presidential elections of 1924, 1928, and 1932. The accuracy of these forecasts was attributed by many people to the sheer size of the sample. However, the *Digest* mailed surveys

[7]After the U.S. Supreme Court intervened to stop recounting, the final official count showed that George W. Bush won Florida by 537 votes out of 5.963 million—or 48.85 percent. Under this count, Gore received 48.84 percent. Florida gave Bush a majority of Electoral College votes.

[8]Exit polls tend to use large stratified, state-specific samples which lowers the margin of error from the standard +/–3 per cent used in major media polls.

[9]Post-election review of uncounted punch cards, "hanging chads," "caterpillar ballots," "butterfly ballots," and illegally counted "overseas" ballots demonstrate that several thousand more people attempted to vote for Gore than Bush in the Florida election. See Jonathan Wand et al, "The Butterfly Did It: The Aberrant Vote for Buchanan in Palm Beach County, Florida," *American Political Science Review*, 95, no. 4 (2001): pp. 793–810. David Barstow and Don Van Natta Jr "How Bush Stole Florida: Mining the Overseas Absentee Ballots" *New York Times* (July 15, 2001). Kosuke Imai and Gary King, "Did Illegally Counted Overseas Ballots Decide the 2000 U.S. Presidential Election?" Manuscript. Department of Government, Harvard University, 2001.

to people drawn from lists of car and telephone owners—a method that ran a serious risk in the 1920s and 1930s of under-representing the less affluent. After surveying more than two million voters in 1936, the *Literary Digest* inferred from its sample that Alf Landon would defeat President Roosevelt, with Landon getting 57 percent of the vote. President Landon? It didn't happen. Landon received only 36 percent of the vote in the election. It should be stressed that a large sample will not necessarily compensate for unrepresentativeness.[10]

Techniques such as stratified random sampling have greatly improved the reliability of polls; however, candidates and interest groups sometimes conduct surveys that replicate the mistakes of the *Digest* polls. Consider the data shown in Table 5.1. During the 1992 presidential campaign, independent candidate Ross Perot's organization mailed out surveys in *TV Guide* magazine and asked readers to mark their ballots as they watched a televised address by the candidate. Responses were then mailed back to Perot's organization. Yet when another group drew random probability samples and respondents were given the same questions, results differed substantially from those reported by the Perot organization.[11] The Perot data suffered from the error of **sample bias**; no real attempts at randomization or stratification were made. Consequently, this poll could not be presented as a credible representation of public opinion.

It should be noted that other sources of error creep into survey research besides the representativeness of the sample. A researcher may have selected a highly representative sample, but his or her instruments of measurement may elicit misleading answers. Common sources of error include those presented in Table 5.2.

---

[10]The 1936 election made George Gallup famous. He used a much smaller and relatively random "quota" sample to predict that Roosevelt would win. For an account of polling in this election, see David W. Moore, *The Superpollsters* (New York: Four Walls Eight Windows, 1992). Gallup's 1936 quota method caused another famous failure, however, when his sample led him to predict that Dewey would defeat Truman in 1948. Since 1948, Gallup and other pollsters have come to use probability samples.

[11]Daniel Goleman, "Pollsters Enlist Psychologists in Quest for Unbiased Results," *New York Times* (September 7, 1993), pp. B5, B8. Also see *The Public Perspective* (Roper Center for Public Research), May/June 1993.

TABLE 5.1   TAXING AND SPENDING:
THE EFFECTS OF SAMPLE BIAS

Question 1: Do you believe that for every dollar of tax increase there should be $2 in spending cuts with the savings earmarked for deficit and debt reduction?

	Yes	No	No Answer
TV Guide Mail-In Response	97%	na	na
Yankelovich National Sample	67	18	15

Question 2: Should laws be passed to eliminate all possibilities of special interests giving huge sums of money to candidates?

	Yes	No	No Answer
TV Guide Mail-In Response	99%	na	na
Yankelovich National Sample	80	17	3

NOTE: "H. Ross Perot Spurs a Polling Experiment (Unintentionally)," from pp. 28–29 by David M. Wilbur, in *Public Perspective*, Vol. 4, #4 © 1993. Reprinted by permission of The Roper Center for Public Opinion Research.

TABLE 5.2   COMMON SOURCES OF ERROR

Error	Example
Ambiguous Questions:	Do you think we ought to strive for peace or for a strong defense?
Symbolically loaded questions that elicit biased answers:	Do you think unborn children have a right to life? Do you think pregnant women should have the right to choose an abortion?
Difficult questions beyond the information level of the respondent:	Do you approve or disapprove of the position on ballistic missile defenses taken by the United States in negotiating the Anti-Ballistic Missile Defense treaty?
Response alternatives unsuited to the subject of the question:	Do you feel better or worse about the future?
Questions that include more than one issue:	Are you more likely to favor a candidate who supports busing and a strong defense or one who has a pleasing personality?

Beyond these obvious kinds of error, some errors arise from the difficulty of being sure you are measuring what you think you are measuring. An example would be a question developed out of an interest in understanding people's personal sympathies for the poor: Do you approve or disapprove of poor people stealing bread when they are hungry? Someone who has enormous sympathy for the poor might say, "I disapprove," because that person, while sympathizing with the poor very strongly, also has enormous respect for law and order. Note that the question is not meaningless; the error comes from attributing an inappropriate meaning to the responses. The question taps another variable, respect for law and order, in addition to the one intended, attitudes toward the poor.[12]

Added to errors arising from sloppy measurement are errors introduced by the statistical procedures used to characterize the data. Statistics always distort reality to at least a small degree—that is why statisticians prefer using several techniques for characterizing data so as to hedge against the bias of a single procedure.

Measuring Relationships between Variables: Association and Correlation
Association

Establishing a degree of **association** between two or more variables gets at the central objective of the scientific enterprise. Scientists spend most of their time figuring out how one thing relates to another and structuring these relationships into explanatory theories.

As with other forms of measurement, the question of association comes up frequently in normal discourse, as in: "like father, like son"; "if you've seen one, you've seen 'em all"; "an orange a

---

[12]An accessible introduction to public opinion polling is Herbert Asher, *Polling and the Public: What Every Citizen Should Know* (Washington, D.C.: CQ Press, 1998).

day keeps the scurvy away." In measuring the degree of association between variables statistically, scientists are merely doing what science is famous for: being rigorous and precise about a commonplace activity.

Association can sometimes be characterized in simple ways. The effects of one variable on another can be described in words or by statistics. "People who use Crust toothpaste have fewer cavities" is a statement that presents a relationship between an independent variable, *brushing with Crust,* and a dependent variable, *number of cavities.*

Descriptive statistics such as the median, the average, and the standard deviation can be employed effectively in specifying association. For example, in our discussion of election systems and voter turnout in chapter two, the percent of voters participating in each nation about was averaged for three different categories of election system (see Table 2.2). This permits analysis of the effect of election system on turnout. Percentage differences are also handy comparative instruments. For example, our discussion of the relationship between social group membership and generations in chapter three (see Table 3.3) showed that just 22 percent of people in the youngest age cohort were members of three or more groups. If there was no relationship between age cohort and group membership, we would expect just 22 percent of people to join three or more groups in every cohort. This isn't the case. Thirty-one percent of people in the older cohorts joined three or more groups—a 9 percent difference.

At this point, we might ask if 9 percent is a big enough difference to say there is a relationship between age cohort and group membership. In this case, the answer is yes. Measures of association and correlation provide us the tools to answer such questions.[13]

---

[13]Given a sample size of 14,259 in Table 3.3, the *chi-square* value for these data is 150.1, which demonstrates that there is a very low probability that group memberships are *independent* of age cohort.

Measures of Association and Correlation

For certain applications, statisticians have developed more sophisticated tools for specifying relationships between variables: measures of association and correlation. Variables measured at different levels require that different statistics be used to test for association. The result is an alphabet soup of tests customarily designated by letters of the Greek alphabet, for example, *chi* and *rho*. All of these tests tend to share a common logic.

Measures of association and correlation are usually approached as a statistical matter; here we will concentrate on the ideas behind them. Our discussion should help you recognize a correlation statistic when you see one. To understand the arithmetic and the limiting assumptions, you may consult a statistics text.

The essential idea of **correlation** is to describe statistically the association between variables. Assuming all other conditions are equal, measures of association summarize the movement of two variables in relation to each other.

Correlation analysis is an advance over comparing percentage differences because it allows you to capture in a single statistic both the *direction* and the *amount* of association. **Direction** refers to whether the association is *positive* or *negative*. A positive correlation exists when, as variable *A* increases, variable *B* also increases. That is, variable *A* goes up as variable *B* goes up (or vice versa). A negative correlation exists when, as variable *A* changes, variable *B* changes in the opposite direction. In the case of a negative correlation, as *A* increases, *B* decreases (or, as *A* decreases, *B* increases).

For example, there is a positive correlation between the quantity of helium in a balloon and the rate at which the balloon rises. There is a negative correlation between the *rate* of rise and the weight attached to the balloon. The positive/negative direction is expressed by a + or − before the correlation figure.

The strength of correlation is expressed by the size of the number on a **scale** from zero to +1.00 or −1.00. The scale is illustrated in Figure 5.2. Thus, correlation statistics provide simple indexes of

FIGURE 5.2　THE SCALE OF CORRELATION

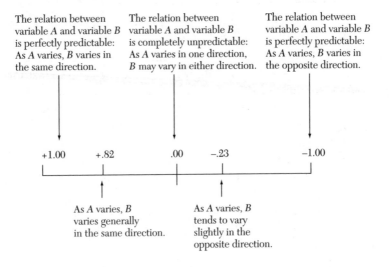

The relation between variable A and variable B is perfectly predictable: As A varies, B varies in the same direction.

The relation between variable A and variable B is completely unpredictable: As A varies in one direction, B may vary in either direction.

The relation between variable A and variable B is perfectly predictable: As A varies, B varies in the opposite direction.

+1.00　　+.82　　　　.00　　−.23　　　　−1.00

As A varies, B varies generally in the same direction.

As A varies, B tends to vary slightly in the opposite direction.

relationships between variables and measures of association—a dangerously simple scheme, for the mathematics behind these statistics involves assumptions that require careful thought. In addition, the variety of techniques by which measures of association are computed causes the results to deviate slightly from the reality of the data. Understanding the general techniques by which correlation operates will allow you to see some, though not all, of the problems. Nevertheless, in the imperfect world of measurement, these statistics are valuable tools.

The techniques for computing measures of association vary with the level of measurement used. If two variables are measured on a nominal scale (classification only), there is less that can be done to characterize association than would be the case with two variables measured on the interval scale. In fact, there are correlation techniques available for every level of measurement, and we will describe generally how they work.

Nominal-Level Association　Nominal measurement, involving only simple classification, is low-grade stuff and the measure of association appropriate to it really doesn't deserve to be called

TABLE 5.3   EXPECTED INCIDENCE OF PLAID WEARING

	Condition of Men	
Pattern of Clothing	*Living*	*Dead*
Plaid	12	12
Non-Plaid	8	8

correlation. The **contingency coefficient** is a statistic often used to summarize how far the actual distribution of data deviates from a distribution in which one variable is associated with no change in the other.

Suppose a researcher wishes to test the proposition stated in the title of an old Steve Martin movie, *Dead Men Don't Wear Plaid*. In order to be thorough, the researcher decides to check on the relative incidence of plaid wearing among the dead as well as living men, to see if being deceased really does make a difference—speaking sartorially. The researcher views a random sample of twenty living men and checks the local funeral parlor for twenty deceased males. If it turns out that men wear plaid just as often alive as dead, then Martin's hypothesis isn't worth much.

Table 5.3 presents a set of results showing no association between wearing plaid and being dead or alive. This is what we might see if there were no association between the two variables. The figures show that twenty-four plaid-wearing men are evenly divided among the living and the dead. Similarly, sixteen non-plaid-wearing men are also as likely living as dead. In this case the contingency coefficient would be zero.

But suppose we actually observe something else. What if there were differences in the amount of plaid wearing among dead men as opposed to living men? How could this be expressed in precise statistical terms?

The contingency coefficient is computed by comparing a distribution of (1) what we would *expect* to see in a table if there were no association (Table 5.3) to (2) what we actually might *observe* (Table 5.4). The results in Table 5.3 can be expressed

TABLE 5.4   OBSERVED INCIDENCE OF PLAID WEARING

| | Condition of Men | |
Pattern of Clothing	*Living*	*Dead*
Plaid	5	14
Non-Plaid	15	6

as either a *chi-square* [pronounced *kye-square*] statistic or a contingency coefficient. Since chi-square has no upper limit, for the sake of interpretation it is often converted into statistics such as the contingency coefficient, with larger values reflecting greater association. If, in fact, the distribution was found as shown in Table 5.3,[14] then chi-square would equal 8.12, and the contingency coefficient would be .41. These statistics point to an association between mortality and clothing—but it isn't the one suggested in the movie title. It appears that a greater proportion of dead men wear plaid than living men.

In more systematic language, this sort of distribution indicates some association between being deceased and wearing a certain pattern of clothing—in this case, plaid. The contingency coefficient is used to characterize the association between non-orderable, nominal-level variables.[15] This measure ranges from −1.0 to +1.0. Remember, a minus statistic indicates that as one variable increases, the other decreases (or vice versa). A plus statistic means that the variation is in the same direction for both variables. When the possibility exists of ordering as well as classifying the categories in the variable, establishing genuine correlation becomes possible.

Ordinal-Level Correlation   "Ordinal" means order. This characteristic supplies the basis for statistics that can be computed at the ordinal level. What can be done is to compare the

---

[14]See G. W. Bohrnstedt and D. Knoke, *Statistics for Social Data Analysis* (Itasca, Ill.: F. E. Peacock, 1988), p. 310.

[15]Other chi-square-based statistics that assess association among variables measured at this level on a scale of zero to one are Cramer's *v* and *phi*.

TABLE 5.5   MUSICAL ABILITY BY SOCIAL CLASS

Ability	Upper Class	Upper Middle Class	Lower Middle Class	Lower Class
Canaries	0	0	5	30
Robins	0	10	20	10
Sparrows	5	15	15	0
Crows	35	15	0	0

ranking of cases according to their ordering on two variables. An illustration will help.

Imagine a group of 160 Boy Scouts singing "God Bless America." The song leader, a systematic person who is secretly a Marxist, rates the singers according to four categories of musical ability from best to worst: Canaries, Robins, Sparrows, and Crows. He wishes to test his belief that lower-class folks are better singers than the upper crust.

So he has two ordered classifications to work with: *musical ability* ordered in terms of Canaries, Robins, Sparrows, and Crows; and *class* ordered in terms of upper, upper middle, lower middle, and lower. The hypothesis he wishes to test is whether there is any association between socioeconomic class and musical ability. The songmaster hypothesizes that lower-class people sing better than upper-class people.

If that were true, the data would show a certain pattern. As class went up, musical ability would go down. The lower classes would be heavily populated with Canaries, and the upper classes with Crows. Suppose he found the distribution presented in Table 5.5.

The relationship is not crystal clear from the data, but we can see that there is a pronounced tendency for lower-class Boy Scouts to warble more sweetly than their "betters." Now we need a statistic that helps nail down the degree of association. Goodman-Kruskal's *gamma*, among other similar statistics, uses an interesting logic to summarize the degree of association. *Gamma* reflects the proportion of reduction in errors in predicting rankings on our dependent variable (musical ability), given knowledge of the ranked distribution of the independent variable (class). If the person's class predicted singing ability perfectly, *gamma* would be high; if not, *gamma* would be low.

Returning to the hypothesis: As we go up the class scale, do the data indicate that there is a corresponding falloff in the musical-ability scale? In the data presented in Table 5.5, the *gamma* would be –0.93. This means that if we know a person's class, it improves our ability of predicting a person's ranking on musical ability by 93 percent (as compared with predicting musical ability knowing nothing about a person's class). Does this affirm the hypothesis? Yes. There is a negative association between class level and ability to sing.

Interval- and Ratio-Level Correlation   To do interval or ratio measurement, you need to be able to establish distances between the units of analysis. It isn't good enough to have singers arrayed in terms of Canaries, Robins, Sparrows, and Crows; the amount of distance between Canaries and Robins and the rest has to be specified. The difference in singing ability between Canaries and Robins may be quite unlike the difference between Sparrows and Crows. With the specification of distance comes the possibility of using a correlation statistic that employs the factor of distance to measure the association between variables.

Interval and ratio measurements allow the use of a formidable-sounding statistic by the name of Pearson's product-moment correlation coefficient, or **Pearson's *r*.**

To keep things simple, we will make up a very elementary example: the relationship between the number of oil wells owned and the number of Cadillacs. Our "sample" consists of five oil well owners. To see what the mathematics of the Pearson's product-moment correlation accomplishes, consider two possible arrays of data. Suppose, first of all, that there is a correlation of +1.00 between number of oil wells and number of Cadillacs. Figure 5.3 illustrates two sets of data for which that same correlation of +1.00 could be claimed.

Notice the straight solid line that can be drawn connecting each case expressing the following relationship between the two

FIGURE 5.3

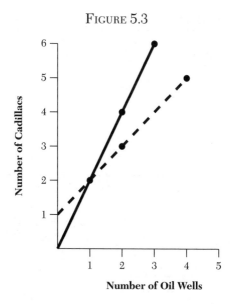

variables: as oil wells increase by one, Cadillacs increase by two. A perfect correlation also results if the straight line should happen to fall on a different level; for example, see the broken line. It shows that you can get a Cadillac without an oil well, but for every extra Cadillac, it appears necessary to sink a new well.

Now imagine an array of data in which the cases do *not* present themselves on a straight line. If the data were to appear as in Table 5.6 and Figure 5.4, no straight line can be drawn that connects all the cases. Imagine that there is one straight line that is closest to all the points on the chart—the line that minimizes the distance by which all the cases deviate from the line. Pearson's *r*, by a mathematical process, identifies how tightly the points cluster around an imaginary line that expresses the linear relationship. For mathematical reasons (best left to mathematicians), the deviations of cases from the line are measured in terms of the squares of the distances $(a^2 + b^2 + c^2 + d^2)$ rather than simple distances $(a + b + c + d)$. The more distant the cases are from the best-fitting line, the lower the correlation of variable *A* with variable *B*. The Pearson's *r* for Figure 5.4 is +.85.

TABLE 5.6   OIL WELLS AND CADILLACS

| Number of Cadillacs | Number of Oil Wells | | | | |
	One	Two	Three	Four	Five
One		1			
Two		1			
Three				1	
Four			1		
Five					1

The Pearson correlation statistic can be made to supply one other important piece of information. By squaring Pearson's r, we can find out what proportion of all the variation in the dependent variable is explained by variation in the independent variable. In the case of oil wells and Cadillacs in Figure 5.4, Pearson's r is +.85, so r^2 is .72 (.85 × .85). Thus, the number of oil wells a person has explains 72 percent of the number of Cadillacs owned. Other variables explain the remaining 28 percent of the variation.

Alternatively, if all of the points fell on the line (as in Figure 5.3) and r is +1.00, then r^2 would also be 1.00 (i.e., 1 × 1 = 1)! The number of oil wells correlates perfectly with the number of Cadillacs, and there is no variation left over to be explained by the other factors.

As with each of the measures of association discussed here, Pearson's r tells us about correlation, which may or may not indicate a causal relationship. A significant r does *not* show that the number of oil wells *causes* people to own more Cadillacs, only that the two things go together. The actual relationship might be reversed (although, in this example, that might seem illogical). We might find that two things are correlated yet have no clear-cut idea about which variable determines the other. Suppose a researcher finds that educational attainment is correlated with intelligence. Which causes which? Measures of association do

FIGURE 5.4

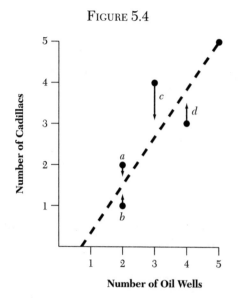

not require that the researcher assume anything about causation. Statistics do not establish causation; *causation depends on the logic of relationships* (see Table 4.4).

Notice what else this procedure does *not* accomplish. A Pearson's *r* of +1.00 indicates only that any variation in *A* is associated with a consistent variation in *B*. What it does *not* tell you is the number of units *B* varies in relation to *A*. It happens in the example in Figure 5.3 (solid line) that as oil wells go up by one, Cadillacs go up by two. But if the situation were such that for *every* increase of one oil well there was a consistent increase of one Cadillac, or 1/2 of a Cadillac, or three Cadillacs, a +1.00 result would be obtained.

In mathematical terms, Pearson's *r* tells you only about the dispersion of cases around an imaginary straight line. It does not tell you the slope of the line—or, in other words, the *amount* of change in *B* for every unit of variation in *A*. A separate statistical procedure involving advanced statistical concepts called *regression analysis* deals with this question.

Regression Analysis

The purposes of this general kind of measurement is to characterize the impact of variables on each other. **Regression analysis** adds a new level of sophistication to these characterizations. With regression, if you know the value of an independent variable, you can begin to predict the value of the dependent variable.

There are two basic forms of regression: *bivariate* regression and *multiple* regression. Bivariate regression, like correlation analysis, characterizes how changes in levels of a single independent variable are related to change in a dependent variable. Multiple regression examines how several different independent variables are associated with a dependent variable.

As an example of bivariate regression, consider a simple example from major-league baseball. Since professional baseball teams spend different amounts of money on player salaries, we might wonder whether higher levels of spending are associated with how a team finishes in the standings. How much of an effect does team payroll have on winning percentage? Bivariate regression helps to answer this question by summarizing the association between the two variables in terms of the following linear equation.

$$Y\ [winning\ percentage] = a + bX[team\ payroll]$$

Expressing the association in words, values of the Y variable (a team's *winning percentage*) are a function of some constant, plus some amount of the X variable. The question we are interested in is if the amount a team spends on its players affects its success on the field. In other words, how much change in the Y variable (*winning percentage*) is associated with a one-unit change in the X variable *(team payroll)*. The answer lies in *b*, the *regression coefficient*.[16]

---

[16]In algebraic terms, *b* represents the slope of the relationship between X and Y. Mixing algebra with baseball, *b* would be the "rise over the run" if we were to plot the relationship between Y and X on a graph.

We can use data from the 2002 baseball season to test the hypothesis that teams with higher payrolls win more games.[17] For each of the thirty major-league teams, we measured *team payroll* (the X variable) as the average a team spent per player, in millions of dollars. We measured *winning percentage* (the Y variable) as the percent of games the team won in 2002. Pearson's r correlation between the two variables is .60, illustrating that as teams spent more money, they won more games. A bivariate regression shows that:

Team winning percentage = 36 + 6.1 × team payroll (in $ millions)

This means that the **slope** of the relationship between a team's payroll and *winning percentage* was 6.1. The result is significant at the .01 level. Put differently, for each million dollars spent on average per player, a team would win 6 percent more games. For a regular baseball season that would be about ten games.

These results show that a team spending an average of $3 million per player would be predicted to win 54.3 percent of their games (36 + 6.1 × $3 million = 54.3 percent, or a .543 record). We can also show that any given team would have to spend over $1.6 million more per player just to increase their winning percentage by 10 percent (36 + 6.1 × $1.64 million = 10.004%).[18]

Modeling winning percentage as being dependent on team payroll explains 36 percent of the variation in winning percentage across the thirty major league teams. This means that other variables—a skilled manager, a strong pitching staff, young talent

[17]Data for team finish were drawn from *http://www.mlb.com*. Data for team payroll were drawn from *http://www.sportingnews.com*.

Baseball writers maintain a curious tradition of reporting a team's record in terms of "percentages," when, in fact, they actually represent proportions. That is, a team is winning when it is over ".500." Our data are recorded as true percentages, so a winning record would be something over 50.0 percent. If we entered proportions into our analysis rather than percentages, b would be expressed in units that would be 100 times smaller.

[18]The *constant* to the intercept of the Y axis (36%) represents what the value of Y would be if X were zero (0)—in this example the percent of games an unpaid team of talented amateurs would be able to win in a season.

that is not paid very much, and other less tangible variables—may be more powerful in explaining why some teams win while others lose.[19] This example from baseball illustrates something we find sometimes in social science: our regression models can leave a great deal unexplained, since some of what we model may be the result of intangibles that are not easily quantified.

Consider another example. In Appendix B, David Brockington, Todd Donovan, Shaun Bowler, and Robert Brischetto explore how a new type of local election system might lead to representation of racial and ethnic minorities. Under standard U.S. "winner-take-all" election rules African-American and Latino residents often have a difficult time getting elected to city councils and school boards. Even in places where a minority group makes up 30 or 40 percent of a community, they can get shut out when white candidates capture majorities and win all the "at-large" seats that are contested citywide. The research question here is straightforward: Do African-Americans and Latinos win seats under alternative "cumulative voting" rules in proportion to their share of a community's population?

Since few U.S. communities adopted cumulative voting rules until the 1990s, there is little previous research on the question. The authors of the study note that theoretically, cumulative voting should produce representation of minorities in rough proportion to their share of a city's population.[20] Previous research established that proportionality could be assessed by using bivariate regression to examine the relationship between the percentage of a community's residents who are minority (the independent variable, or X) and the percentage of council seats held by minorities (dependent variable, or Y).

---

[19]Since Pearson's r for this example was .60, we know that spending explains 36 percent of variation in team winning percentages ($.60 \times .60 = .36$). One reason that the *model fit* represented by r^2 is just .36 is that a number of teams with below-average payrolls had the best records in 2002 (the Anaheim Angels and the Oakland A's), while a couple of teams with high payrolls had poor records (the Texas Rangers and the New York Mets).

[20]Under cumulative voting, a voter may cast as many votes as there are seats contested. If four seats are up for election, a person could vote for one candidate four times, four candidates one time, and so on. For a discussion, see Lani Guinier, *Lift Every Voice* (New York: Simon & Schuster, 1998).

The authors of the study found that the slope of the relationship for places with African-American minorities is 0.95, with a Y-intercept near zero (see Table 2 in Appendix B). This means that in places using cumulative voting, a 1 percent increase in the African-American population is associated with a 0.95 percent increase in the proportion of council seats held by African Americans. In other words, representation is close to proportional. In Figures 1 and 2 in Appendix B, this relationship is displayed graphically. The authors compare their results to those from other regression analyses of minority representation. They illustrate that in the South, these new cumulative voting rules may produce even more minority representation than do election systems that rely on the use of racially homogeneous districts.

What about regression that involves more than one variable (and what about an example that relates directly to politics?). As an example of **multiple regression**, suppose you notice that your friends differ widely in their level of involvement in electoral politics. Activity might range across a spectrum as illustrated here:

nonvoters   occasional voters   party activists

Why are some people more active than others? Factors that occur prior to, or independently of, activism would include income levels, education levels, or levels of prior experience with politics (call them independent variables). Each could logically be associated with the level of activism. Multiple regression permits analysis of the effects of several independent variables at the same time. This technique isolates the effect of a single independent variable while controlling for (or holding constant) the effects of other independent variables.

To pursue the example, political activism, the dependent variable, could be operationalized in terms of a score derived from the number of political activities a person is involved in: voting, campaigning, contributing to candidates, engaging in protests or demonstrations, and so on. The more activities engaged in, the higher the participation score. For the sake of simplicity, let's assume our measure of political activism ranges from zero to ten.

As we have seen, measures of correlation make it possible to see whether income and political participation, for example, are positively or negatively related (whether participation goes up or down as income rises). Correlation also establishes how closely one varies in association with the other.

With a knowledge of the correlation of income and participation, you can estimate whether a rich person is more or less likely to be politically active than a poor person. If, however, you would like to have a better chance of predicting the amount of change in participation associated with each change in level of income, then regression analysis is required. To test for the effect of one independent variable on a dependent variable while controlling for the effects of one or more additional variables, multiple regression is required.

For example, we might expect that variation in political activism is associated with both income and education. Multiple regression estimates statistically the unique effect of each variable on the dependent variable while holding other independent variables constant. Thus, we can see if education affects participation while controlling for income levels. Multiple regression tables typically report a series of b's (slopes, or regression coefficients) for each of the independent variables included in the analysis. These are interpreted as the amount of change in the dependent (Y) variable associated with a one-unit change in an independent variable (X_1) holding other included variables (X_2, X_3, etc.)

Recall the brief discussion about control and spuriousness from chapter four. Social scientists are often unable to use laboratories to control or "hold constant" the effects of multiple variables. It would be impossible as well as cruel, for example, to randomly distribute certain levels of income and education to different people, then place them under observation and wait to see whether participation occurs at different rates among people with different mixes of income and education. For this reason, social scientists often measure existing phenomena and then use statistical procedures such as multiple regression to control for the effects of variables that cannot (or should not) be manipulated.[21]

Interpreting multiple regression coefficients can become awkward when the independent variables are measured in different units. Since measures of income (dollars) range much more widely than measures of education (years of schooling) it is hard to compare regression coefficients for the two variables. But there is a statistical technique for making them comparable. The units can be expressed in terms of *standard deviation* units.

A "normally" distributed variable has about two thirds of all observations fall somewhere within one standard deviation above or below the mean. Extreme scores lie two or three deviations above or below the mean.

A variable that has a lot of cases that are at the high and low ends of variation, regardless of how great the range of variation is, will have large standard deviation. A variable for which the scores concentrate around the average will have a low standard deviation. This method of standardizing is used often in regression analysis.[22]

The resulting standardized regression coefficient is typically referred to as the **beta coefficient;** like Pearson's *r*, it usually varies from −1.00 to +1.00. In terms of the dependent variable in our example, political activism, if we found that the Beta coefficient for income was +1.00, this would indicate that a one-standard-deviation-unit change in income is associated with a one-standard-deviation-unit change in participation.

---

[21]A treatment of the mathematics of regression is beyond the scope of this book, but countless texts are available on the topic. Brief, accessible introductions can be found in L. Schroeder, D. Sjoquist, and P. Stephan, *Understanding Regression Analysis,* Sage University Paper Series on Quantitative Applications in the Social Sciences, no. 57 (Beverly Hills, Calif.: Sage Publications, 1986); or M. Lewis-Beck, *Applied Regression,* Sage University Paper Series on Quantitative Applications in the Social Sciences, no. 22 (Beverly Hills, Calif.: Sage Publications, 1980).

[22]A number of technical problems are associated with using standardized regression coefficients. Some scholars suggest that findings should simply be expressed in terms of "real" units. See Gary King, "How Not to Lie with Statistics," *American Journal of Political Science* 30, no. 3 (1986):666–687.

If we found the Beta to be +.50, web would conclude that a one-standard-deviation-unit change in income is associated with a one-half-standard-deviation change in participation.

The regression coefficient and the Beta coefficient are one part of regression analysis. The other part is a multiple correlation statistic, R (not to be confused with Pearson's small r, which deals with a single independent variable). R reports the correlation between a group of independent variables and a dependent variable. In parallel fashion there is R^2 which indicates the proportion of the variation in the dependent variable explained by the group of dependent variables under consideration.

Putting this all together, if we used a computer statistics package to conduct a multiple regression analysis of the effects that income and education had on political activism, our results would include b, and *beta* for each independent variable, as well as R^2, which describes the effects of all the independent variables. Since we have two independent variables in our example, we would have two unique b's or slopes, and two unique *betas*. The b's are expressed in whatever units the dependent variable is measured in. So, if b for education was .25, this would mean that every one unit change in education is associated with a quarter-point increase on our political activism score—with the effects of income held constant. If the *beta* for education was .10, this means that a one standard deviation unit increase in education is associated with a .10 standard deviation increase in activism. If $R^2 = .56$, we would know that the two variables explain just over half of the variation in our political activism measure.

As a way of summarizing what has been presented so far about measuring relationships between variables and to set the agenda for the remaining discussion, look at Table 5.7.

Why Multiple Regression?
Control and Spuriousness

How do you establish the unique effect of one independent variable while the effects of others are held constant? Multiple regression analysis is the answer.

TABLE 5.7   MEASURES OF ASSOCIATION, CORRELATION,
AND REGRESSION

Statistic[a]	Meaning
r	*Pearson's correlation coefficient:* the degree of covariance between two variables (-1.00 to $+1.00$)
r^2	*Coefficient of determination:* in bivariate regression, the proportion of the variation in a dependent variable explained by the changes in the independent variable (0 to $+1.00$)
R	*Multiple correlation statistic:* the degree of covariance in a dependent variable associated with changes in two or more independent variables (0 to $+1.00$)
R^2	*Coefficient of determination:* the proportion of the variation in a dependent variable explained by changes in two or more independent variables (0 to $+1.00$)
b	*Unstandardized regression coefficient:* the amount of variation in a dependent variable that occurs with each unit of variation in the independent variable (zero to infinity)
beta	*Standardized regression coefficient:* the amount of variation in a dependent variable for each unit of variation in one or more independent variables where the units of all variables are made comparable in terms of standard deviations from the mean (usually varies between -1.00 and $+1.00$)

[a]For purposes of this table, we are using Pearson's r as the the only measure of correlation. For other measures, see footnote 2 in this chapter.

Recall in chapter three, that scholars studying social capital are interested in how memberships in voluntary groups is associated with political participation. In Appendix A, Robert Putnam provides evidence that low levels of group membership are associated with high levels of television viewing. He writes "Even after controlling for education, income, age, race, place of residence, work status, and gender, TV viewing is strongly and negatively related to social trust and group membership."

Figure X in Appendix A provides a visual illustration of how social scientists test if the unique effect of one variable on another—in this example the effect of television viewing on joining groups—holds when the effect of another variable is accounted for. In the example from Putnam, we can see that people who watch the *least* TV join the *most* groups *at every level of education.* In other words, the negative relationship between watching TV and joining groups remains even after we control for the effect of education.

Putnam wants to isolate one variable as the prime suspect to explain the decline of social capital in America. In Appendix A, much of the evidence points to television as the culprit. By controlling for many possible rival explanations, he can make a stronger claim that the deleterious effect of TV is not due to another factor that is not accounted for. This is the problem of spuriousness.

A result is said to be spurious if it can be explained away by another variable. A classic example of a spurious relationship is the high correlation between the *number of fire trucks* at the scene of the fire and the *amount of damage* caused by the fire. The conclusion seems simple: additional trucks cause more damage! The omitted variable, of course, is the *size of the fire.* A bigger fire brings out more trucks *and* causes more damage.

To return to the question of social capital, what if frequent television viewers were people who simply had less time or energy to join social groups? It could be that many people now work longer hours, or spend more time commuting. By the time they get home it may be too late to meet with any groups. This being so, they end up spending their evenings watching TV. From this perspective, TV viewing is not the main cause of the decline of social capital. Rather, it may be a variable that corresponds with another important variable (lack of free time) that causes people to forgo joining social groups.

One fundamental goal of any scientific endeavor is to control for other variables that might explain away an important result. In your own research you might not use advanced statistics or laboratory experiments to control for any or all omitted variables that could explain away your observations. Nevertheless, you should consider how confident you are that your results are not spurious.

To take the discussion a few steps further, let's look at another example. Table 5.8 is taken from a study by Susan Welch, Michael Combs, and John Gruhl. They explore the question,

TABLE 5.8   THE IMPACT OF A JUDGE'S RACE ON SENTENCE
SEVERITY AND THE DECISION TO INCARCERATE

	Decision to Incarcerate		Sentence Severity		
	MLE	MLE/SE	b	beta	t
All Defendants					
No controls	.10	2.10°	−.48	−.01	−.67
Controls for defendant and crime	.14	2.17°	−.91	−.02	−1.60
Controls for judge, defendant, and crime	.11	1.67	−1.22	−.03	−2.14°
White Defendants					
No controls	.11	.92	.27	.01	.20
Controls for defendant and crime	.35	2.19°	1.40	.04	1.31
Controls for judge, defendant, and crime	.35	2.18°	1.39	.04	1.30
Black Defendants					
No controls	.10	1.72	−.80	−.02	−.96
Controls for defendant and crime	.09	1.24	−1.59	−.04	−2.40°
Controls for judge, defendant, and crime	.06	.78	−2.00	−.05	−2.99°

CODING: Black judges = 1, white judges = 0. Controls for defendant and crime include the severity of the crime, whether the defendant pled guilty, the defendant's prior record, and whether or not he had a public defender. Additional controls for judicial characteristics include the judge's prosecutorial experience, sex, and years on the bench. N = 3,418 for all defendants, 763 for white defendants, and 2,655 for black defendants. ° = significant at .05.
NOTE: MLE is the Maximum Likelihood Estimate, and SE is the Standard Error.
SOURCE: Susan Welch, Michael Combs, and John Gruhl, "Do Black Judges Make a Difference?" *American Journal of Political Science* 32, no. 1 (1988):126–136.

"Do black judges make a difference?" They examine the factors that affect trial judges' sentencing decisions. The authors wanted to know whether white judges treat criminal defendants differently than do black judges. The research question here is straightforward: Do sentencing decisions depend upon a judge's race?

Previous research was inconclusive—different studies found contradictory results. The authors noticed that earlier researchers failed to control for such important independent variables as the *severity of the defendant's crime, the defendant's previous record*, and other characteristics of the judge (such as *gender*).

Welch et al. develop their data from a sample of male defendants convicted of felonies between 1968 and 1979 in a large northeastern city. In one part of the analysis, they operationalize their dependent variable as the severity of the judge's sentence. They use a severity scale where 0 equals a suspended sentence; lower scores reflect fines and probation; higher scores reflect jail time; and the highest value, 93, equals life imprisonment. Because they wanted to control for multiple independent variables, they used multiple regression analysis.

Using a form of bivariate regression, they find that the judge's race (the independent variable) is *not* associated with sentence severity. That is, when they look only at the relationship between the judge's race and the severity of sentence, there is no relationship.[23] But when multiple regression is used and they introduce controls for severity of the defendant's crime and other factors, they find a significant, albeit slight, difference.[24] Black judges are associated with a sentence that is 1.22 units lower on the severity scale of 0 to 93. This effect is particularly evident when the sample examined is limited to black defendants. Compared to white judges, black judges' sentences of black defendants are exactly two units lower in severity—however, there is more to the story.[25]

Probit and Logit Analysis

Welch and her colleagues also note that severity of sentencing is not the only aspect, or even the most critical aspect, of judicial sentencing decisions. Prior to deciding about the severity of the sentence, the judge must decide whether the defendant

[23]Beta = –.01, b = –0.48; not significant.
[24]Beta = –.03., b = –1.22.
[25]Beta = –.05. b = –2.00.

will or will not be incarcerated. Some people are let off with probation, and although convicted of a felony, they are not required to spend time in jail.

When the dependent variable is conceived in these terms, regression analysis cannot be applied. Correlation and regression analysis assume that the dependent variable is measured at the interval or ordinal level. *Decision to incarcerate*, however, is coded such that 1 = incarcerate, 0 = do not incarcerate. This being the case, we cannot talk about how a one-unit change in independent variable produces a change of some number of units in the dependent variable.

Another form of analysis similar to multiple regression is designed to deal with these dichotomous (two-category) dependent variables.[26] Social science researchers often deal with dependent variables that are simple nominal categories such as "yes or no" survey questions, or how various factors affect a government's decision to adopt a public policy or fight in a war. **Probit and logit analysis** are being used with increasing frequency to address these questions.

Rather than producing regression coefficients or Betas, probit produces a coefficient that is not easily interpretable on its own. With the aid of a mathematical formula (omitted here for simplicity's sake), these coefficients can be used to assess how changes in X affect the *probability* that Y will assume one value or the other. This statistic can help answer the question as to whether a difference in the judge's race affects the probability that a felon will serve time in jail.[27]

---

[26]The procedure is referred to as probit or logit analysis, or "logistic regression" in some cases. Probit and logit differ slightly in the assumptions made about the underlying distribution of the dependent variable. See J. Aldrich and F. Nelson, *Linear Probability, Logit and Probit Models*, Sage University Paper Series on Quantitative Applications in the Social Sciences, no. 45 (Beverly Hills, Calif.: Sage Publications, 1984).

[27]When correlation and regression are used to test for a relationship, the statistics test how well the data are represented by a straight line or slope. When probit analysis is used, the statistic tests how well the relationship between X and Y is represented by an S-shaped curve. A statistic that searches for a linear association (correlation and regression) between the *decision to incarcerate* (Y) and the *severity of the crime* (X) might miss the relationship and lead to many errors in prediction.

Welch et al. use probit analysis to test the relationship between the independent variables and the decision to incarcerate.[28] They find that black judges are more likely to decide to incarcerate defendants than white judges. However, when the authors control for other variables, the significance of this effect disappears.

The probit analysis also shows that there are significant racial differences in the decision to incarcerate white defendants once controls for other factors are introduced into the analysis. White defendants are less likely to be sent to prison when sentenced by white judges; put differently, black judges are more likely to sentence white defendants to jail when severity of the crime and other factors are accounted for.

Welch and her colleagues conclude, after assessing all of the measures, that black judges do make a difference in the criminal justice system. Based on the results of the multiple regression and probit analysis of this particular sample, black judges appear slightly more likely than white judges (1) to sentence white defendants to prison, and (2) to give slightly less severe sentences to black defendants. However, "in the decision about incarceration, black judges appear even-handed [as between black and white defendants], while white judges are less likely to send whites than blacks to jail."[29] Note that the authors qualify their results and make an effort to explain the multiple factors that might explain why blacks and whites behave differently.

As a way of summarizing what has been presented so far about measuring relationships between variables, see Table 5.9.

The central problem in regression has to do with sorting out the interrelated or statistically overlapping effects of several independent variables on the dependent variable. The problem can be attacked, though rarely resolved completely, by precise operationalization, by analysis of the covariance of similar independent variables, and by such techniques as probit analysis.

---

[28]In Welch et al., "Do Black Judges Make a Difference?," Table 1, the probit coefficients are referred to as MLEs (maximum likelihood estimates). Welch et al. deem the coefficient significant if it is at least twice the size of its standard error (MLE/SE > 2.0).

[29]Welch et al., p. 134.

TABLE 5.9   MEASUREMENTS OF RELATIONS BETWEEN VARIABLES

Correlation	The degree of association or covariation between two interval- or ratio-level variables. Direction of the relationship is indicated by the plus or minus sign.
Bivariate Regression	The amount of change in an interval- or ratio-level dependent variable associated with a one-unit change in a single independent variable.
Multiple Regression	The amount of change in an interval- or ratio-level dependent variable explained by several variables. Tests for the unique effect of each independent variable. Used in conjunction with R^2, which reports the proportion of variation in the dependent variable explained by the independent variables acting together.
Probit and Logit Analysis	A form of multiple regression wherein the dependent variable is dichotomous (e.g., yes/no; for/against). Examines how a unit change in an independent variable will produce a change in the probability that the dependent variable will take one value or the other.

In any multiple regression model or probit analysis, a good many technicalities, precautions, and limiting assumptions need to be considered before the results are taken seriously. However, the logic of the analysis is what we are after here. Several variables affect judicial decisions. The researchers' logic suggests that some of these variables need to be accounted for, or controlled for statistically in order that they might make conclusions about a variable they are particularly interested in: *race*. In the example, it appears that there are some significant effects of race, even after we control for other factors such as severity of the crime.

As technical as the statistics make it seem, regression and probit analysis, like science in general, begin with creativity and imagination. The first part of regression analysis involves figuring out which variables to test for—and this comes from an awareness of theory and a keen sense of the subject under investigation. The usefulness of regression analysis is that it indicates the possibilities for even more precise measurement of relations between variables in hypotheses.

Computers and Statistics

The development of statistical software for computers makes it possible for researchers to process data quickly and efficiently. A certain amount of mathematical and conceptual background used to be the prerequisite for the calculation of statistics. Now computers can do the mathematics. In some instances, this means that data are manipulated in ways that are not appropriate to level of measurement.

Although it is possible to leave the mathematics to a computer, it is dangerous to use statistical techniques without being fully aware of the conceptual foundations for mathematical processes. Just because a software package can produce a correlation statistic for two variables doesn't mean that the measurement standards necessary for correlation have been met. It is tempting to resort to software-produced statistics that seem to offer great precision; however there is no substitute for a careful assessment of the properties and characteristics of the data according to the guidelines suggested here (see Figure 5.1).

Statistics don't create data; they describe it. Just as it would be nonsensical to describe something abstract by referring to its color or other physical properties, so is it misleading to claim statistical relationships where none can be calculated.

The refinements we have discussed are themselves just the beginnings of what can be done to elaborate and improve research strategies. We have sought only to map the major pathways of understanding and technique. Further development of research skills usually comes not so much from forced marches through methodology texts as from the motivation generated by an interesting project. As the project develops, methodological matters become more significant and more rewarding to learn.

In pursuing methodological understanding, however, beware of a simple "cookbook" approach. Understand the idea of what you are doing before enlisting the specific techniques by which it can be accomplished. That, at least, is the bias of this book and the experience of its authors. The wealth of detail found in the technical literature on methodology becomes much more digestible if the relatively simple ideas that underlie the calculations can be seen. Ideas provide frameworks for the mechanics of technique.

• CONCEPTS INTRODUCED

Measurement	Descriptive statistics
Properties of variables	Correlation
Nominal	Direction of association
Ordinal	Scale of correlation
Interval	Contingency coefficient
True zero	Pearson's *r*
Ratio	Regression analysis
Arbitrary zero	Slope
Probability	Multiple regression
Level of significance	Standard deviation
Probability sample	Beta coefficient
Stratification	*R*
Random sampling	R^2
Sampling bias	Probit and logit analysis
Association	

• QUESTIONS FOR DISCUSSION

1. Recall that samples are used to estimate something about a larger population. Considering this, how might the sampling technique and method used to gather the Perot data cause the results to be biased?

2. Examine the questions in Table 5.1 taken from the Perot survey. How might the wording of the questions introduce errors in measuring the attitudes of respondents?

3. Can we think of a more neutral wording for the Perot survey questions? How/why would neutral wording create a measure that better taps attitudes of the population?

4. Is a baseball team's division finish (place in the division) an interval-variable that taps the concept of *team performance* well? What would be a better interval-level measure of a team's performance?

5. Look at Figure 1 in the Brockington et al. article (Appendix B) What would the line representing the relationship between minority population and minority seat share look like if the regression coefficient (or slope) was only 0.25? What would it look like if it was 1.5? What is the substantive meaning of larger or smaller slope?

PREVIEW OF CHAPTER SIX

- Factuality, Reality, and Actuality
- Morality and the Limits of Science
- Of Scientists, Science, and Paradigms
- Making Social Science Serve Human Needs
- The Radicalism of Science
- Science and Politics

REFLECTIONS: BACK TO THE ROOTS

"**Knowledge joined to power represents nothing less than the history of life itself. . . .**"

—JOHN PATRICK DIGGINS

Our brief study began with the very foundations of knowing: the emergence of language concepts from elementary human experience. Now the structure of method raised in this foundation can, with the aid of insights gained by our look at the operational side of science, be addressed in a more sophisticated manner. It is time to put science itself into the perspective of a broader understanding. We need to know a little more of how science fits within a larger perspective on knowledge, how scientists relate to science, and finally, how each of us can use science as a means of increasing our ability to deal with our own environment.

Factuality, Reality, and Actuality

The scientific method often appears at first as a kind of narrow restrictive way of reaching understanding. The demands for precision are rigorous, the statistics forbidding, and, all too often, the results difficult to read. At the same time, zealous defenders of science sometimes indiscreetly claim for science more than it can support as a strategy of knowledge. Feigning a mythical objectivity, they confuse the procedures of science for testing hypotheses with a claim to personal and professional immunity from bias and prejudice.

In trying to gain perspective on science, we can learn something from one of this century's major theorists of the human condition, Erik Erikson. In the course of his experience as a psychoanalyst, his research on various subcultures, and his extensive studies of crucial personalities in history, Erikson came to characterize understanding as multidimensional. Erikson distinguishes between three dimensions of our relationship to the world around us: *factuality, reality,* and *actuality*.[1] Science, as we will see, is involved with each of these dimensions.

Of the three, **factuality** fits most closely with the popular view of scientific methodology. *Factuality is that "universe of facts, data, and techniques that can be verified with the observational methods and the work techniques of the time."*[2]

Much of what we have been considering here deals with the effort to establish that elusive item of inquiry, the fact. Earlier we hinted at a personal dislike for the word *fact*. By now, however, enough has been said to make it clear that facts are not to be confused with Truth. A fact is only as good as the means of verification used to establish it, as well as the frame of reference within

---

[1]See Erik Erikson, *Gandhi's Truth* (New York: Norton, 1969), p. 396; *Dimensions of a New Identity* (New York: Norton, 1974), pp. 33–34; and *Life History and the Historical Moment* (New York: Norton, 1975), pp. 103–104. Erikson's formulations of these concepts vary somewhat, and we have adapted them to suit the purposes of this exposition. For a fascinating account of how Erikson developed his analysis, see Lawrence Friedman, *Erik Erikson: Identity's Architect* (New York: Scribner's, 1999).

[2]Erikson, *Dimensions of a New Identity*, p. 33, italic ours.

which it acquires meaning. A great deal of science consists of using methodological advances to revise, modify, or even falsify "facts" and theories formerly "verified" by cruder or less sensitive techniques. By trying to verify observations systematically, we strengthen the bridge between our perceptions of the world and phenomena outside ourselves.

All the concern with thoughtful variable specification, precise measurement, and cautious interpretation of results has to do both with developing data worthy of being called factual *and* with understanding the limits of such data. Although the factual view of the world seldom seems to have the glamour or subtlety of, say, the poetic view, we have tried to establish that it has a power and social utility of its own. Factuality is a necessary component of our world view, though the limitations on creating factual information, and the human characteristics we bring to the task, require a broader perspective on knowledge.

Reality, the second of the dimensions, or aspects, of understanding, is seemingly less concrete but perhaps intuitively quite simple. Our sense of what constitutes reality is not merely a summation of factuality. *What we know as reality is, rather, a perspective on factuality integrated by the sense in which we understand these things.* Given the limitations of fact-gathering technique, the pressures of the moment, and the unconscious elements in the background of our understanding, we have to be aware that no matter how hard we try, our understanding will never be exclusively factual. Nor need it be. Science is a discipline for finding and organizing evidence about what interests us. We then try to use that evidence to shape our view of reality. Consequently, we can legitimately ask of those who engage in science that they convey to us not just the "facts" but something of their sense of the realities reflected in their data.

A science that is to be social must engage in a kind of balancing act between the scientific principle that statements must be verified and, on the other hand, the social necessity for doing something about the crises of civilization. Verification of social theory often lags behind the necessities of social policy. In bringing together the verified and the speculative through an insightful sense of reality, we increase the possibility of an informed understanding of the world—and of our ability to change it. Developing this kind of approach to reality is no simple matter, nor can we say exactly how it comes about—except that personal commitment, experience, a willingness to suspend preconceived ideas, and good scientific procedure all play a part.

Factuality, the world of data and observation, and a sense of reality, the perspective in which we understand evidence, do not yet constitute the world of knowledge. Erikson suggests a third dimension of existence, *actuality*, which for our purposes means *knowledge gained in and through action*.

Science creates an image of reflective inquiry, of the researcher observing phenomena to gather information and then retreating to some quiet place to assemble, digest, and characterize what can be known. Yet such a detached mode of understanding is not typical of most of us. Human beings are, it seems, more oriented to action than reflection. **Actuality** has something to do with how we act on (or transact between) the modes of our knowing and the occasions for behavior.

Erikson illustrates his concept of actuality by discussing his own experience as a psychoanalyst. Psychoanalysis is basically a creative form of behavioral inquiry. Erikson comments that therapy is never really a process by which a doctor prescribes some course of action to a patient, but rather a *mutual* exploration to which the psychoanalyst brings training and experience, and the patient a personal history, deep feelings, and capacities for insights and action. The psychoanalytic encounter matches *potentialities* between doctor and patient.

The same can be said for social scientific inquiry. The behavior we study does not simply lie there on a slide plate or bubble in a test tube; it is formed out of the same animating principles that move the researcher as a person. The best social scientists are those who become engaged by the behavior they study. They use rigorous analysis, but they also reach into action itself as a source of understanding.

Social scientists are circumspect about the question of personal involvement in the behavior they study. The obvious reason is that disciplined thought can be hard enough to achieve, without intruding on the feelings evoked by becoming engaged. Yet all social inquiry consists of a personal transaction with something outside ourselves. As a personal stance, detachment has its disadvantages just as involvement does. Whatever strategy is adopted, good inquiry really calls for a very high level of consciousness. *The scientific method makes conscious and explicit that part of the transaction dealing with the verification of observations.* There is a similar need to be highly conscious of how one's own experience and personality enter into the task of understanding.[3]

Aside from forcing a recognition of the personal elements of inquiry, Erikson suggests that experimental involvement opens up potentialities for insight. Behavior is reflexive; it emerges through transactions with an environment. Understanding the transactions experienced in an environment requires a "feel" for what is human about behavior. Such understanding demands an appreciation of factuality and a perspective on reality, but also a sense of action and what it can reveal.

Lately there has been increasing interest in what are now called **observational studies.** These studies try to capture a much larger proportion of the reality that is being studied. Open-ended interviews, evocative descriptions of the surroundings, and direct reporting of personal experience characterize this approach. Behind the apparent storylike quality of observational studies is usually a thoughtful effort to test some theories and

---

[3]Some classics of social science owe their particular value to the personal involvement of the authors in their subject matter—for example, Floyd Hunter, *Community Power Structure* (New York: Doubleday, 1963); Robert Lane, *Political Ideology: Why the American Common Man Believes What He Does* (New York: Free Press, 1962); C. Wright Mills, *The Power Elite* (New York: Oxford University Press, 1959); and William Foote Whyte, *Street Corner Society* (Chicago: University of Chicago Press, 1943).

provide evidence for hypotheses. The science is not so much in variable specification and the measurement of relationships as in locating the crucial observations and drawing out their theoretical implications.[4]

Every student has gone through the process of learning something intellectually and then relearning it through experience. Science is recommended as the mode of knowing that will most benefit one's ability to establish facts, to understand the reality surrounding them, and to approach actuality with sensitivity.

Science is more an attitude and a set of general guidelines than a specific strategy. There are many possible research strategies for getting at the various levels of factuality, reality, and actuality. The choice of strategies is part of the challenge.[5]

Feminist scholars have developed new perspectives on social science methodology that open up a broader range of strategies for thinking about evidence. Drawing on studies that point to significant differences in the psychological development of women and men, these scholars suggest that female approaches to the relational character of human society need to be incorporated into social scientific research designs. Techniques that rigidly control the definition of data and establish boundaries for categorizing responses to surveys, for example, need to be supplemented by long interviews and other forms of qualitative evidence

[4]For some resources on these methods, see Herbert Blumer, ed., "The Methodological Position of Symbolic Interaction," *Symbolic Interactionism: Perspective and Method* (Englewood Cliffs, N.J.: Prentice-Hall, 1969), pp. 1–60); Howard S. Becker, "Problems of Inference and Proof in Participant Observation," *American Sociological Review* 23 (1958): 652–660; George McCall, "The Problem of Indicators in Participant Observation Research," *Issues in Participant Observation*, ed. George McCall and J. L. Simmons (Reading Mass.: Addison-Wesley, 1969), pp. 230–239; and John Lofland, *Analyzing Social Settings* (Belmont, Calif.: Wadsworth, 1973).

[5]Some sources that will help with the problem of choosing between research strategies are Morris Zelditch, Jr., "Some Methodological Problems in Field Studies," *American Journal of Sociology* 67 (March 1962): 566–576; Donald Warwick, "Survey Research and Participant Observation: A Benefit-Cost Analysis," *Comparative Research Methods*, ed. Donald Warwick and Samuel Asherson (Englewood Cliffs, N.J.: Prentice-Hall, 1973), pp. 189–203; and Davydd Greenwood, William Foote Whyte, and Ira Harkevy, "Participatory Action Research in a Process and as a Goal," *Human Relations* 46, no. 2 (1993): 175–192.

gathering. In this view, studies that evoke the interdependent nature of human relationships, whether through qualitative or quantitative observations, should become a significant part of any social inquiry.[6]

Morality and the Limits of Science

As the preceding discussion suggests, science does not answer all questions, and the answers it does provide must be placed in the perspective of other forms of understanding. In other words, science has its limitations. It is time to make these limitations explicit.

A concern for moral values that allow human beings to coexist in a civilized and peaceful fashion requires that we accept limits on how social science research is carried on, and on what is done with the results. A regard for prudence as well as ethics requires that we limit the claims of scientific knowledge in view of what it *cannot* demonstrate and that we acknowledge the possibility that other strategies of knowledge may provide better answers. Each of these topics is worth further examination.

Taking a scientific approach to human behavior involves two major kinds of moral issues. The manipulation of people in research projects can be very risky to the individuals involved, and the results of scientific research can be used to exploit rather than to benefit people.

A famous example of the moral difficulties of manipulating experimental subjects is the Milgram experiments on obedience to authority.[7] The experiments required volunteers, under the

[6]See Sandra Harding, *Feminism and Methodology* (Bloomington: Indiana University Press, 1987); and Carol Gilligan, *In a Different Voice: Psychological Theory and Women's Development* (Cambridge, Mass.: Harvard University Press, 1982). For an interesting example of the use of these ideas in research, see Rand Jack and Dana Jack, *Moral Vision and Professional Decisions: The Changing Values of Women and Men Lawyers* (New York: Cambridge University Press, 1989).

[7]Stanley Milgram, *The Individual in a Social World* (Reading, Mass.: Addison-Wesley, 1977).

direction of "scientific researchers," to administer electric shocks to "students" in order to encourage them to learn material that they were studying. The volunteers were told that the experiment had to do with testing a method for teaching people certain kinds of material more effectively. But the real point of the experiment was to test people's obedience to authority figures, in this case social scientific researchers. Unbeknownst to the volunteers, the electric shocks were phony, and the behavior of the volunteers themselves was the real subject of the experiment. There was a lot of deception involved here. The experiment was later explained to the volunteers, and some were provided with follow-up counseling. A number of the volunteers were deeply upset to find that they had been willing to administer ostensibly dangerous electrical shocks to people in a blind response to professional authority.

Wrap the flag around an overzealous scientist and there is the possibility of a real disaster. The use of unsuspecting human subjects in determining the effects of radiation from nuclear emissions and bomb tests is a case in point. The U.S. government is now attempting to find out who was harmed and how they can be compensated.

The purpose of social science should be to improve the quality of human life. That noble end does not justify the use of means that degrade human life, either by deceiving people into doing something they would seriously regret under normal circumstances, or by exposing their inner motivations without taking responsibility for the results to the individual. Social scientists must be truthful with the subjects of experiments and obtain their informed consent as a condition of participation.

While the ethics of dealing with experimental subjects is a matter under the control and responsibility of the researcher, a much more difficult moral problem arises when we consider the exploitative potential of social science research. The debate over the uses of social science takes place in the shadow of the controversy concerning those scientists who did the original research for atomic weapons in the 1940s. Their argument was that they were pursuing the path of science—the *uses* of science being the province of others. Although social scientists have no atomic bombs to show for their efforts, the technology of social control that social science has begun to generate may well come to have a power of a magnitude worthy of the same moral concern.

We can't resolve these moral debates here, except to suggest that the cause of advancing science has no special ethical standing. To do something in the name of science doesn't excuse anybody from the moral considerations that make humane living possible.

The moral considerations discussed here do limit the kind of research that can be done in good conscience. Another limitation comes not from ethical considerations as applied to science but from the very nature of science itself. Remember that science begins—and also ends—in uncertainty.[8] What science does is *reduce* uncertainty, but ultimately it cannot *eliminate* it. Were this possible, scientists would be gods rather than humans.

People disagree whether there are gods, and science can't settle the issue. The scientific method is merely a tool humans can use to try to reduce the inevitable uncertainty with which we all live. Humans are themselves observers of limited capacity, and the techniques and tools that science uses are imperfect. That is the reason for the emphasis on explicit evidence and the replication of findings.

The point is that true scientists generalize where there is evidence, but they do not claim more than the evidence allows. They certainly do not deny the possibility that other forms of knowledge (e.g., faith, intuition, or custom) may embody wisdom beyond the reach of evidence as scientists understand it. Scientists can and should use techniques of evidence to test the claims made by these other forms of knowledge. There are good results to show for the effort, as any inspection of medical history, for example, will demonstrate. Yet there remain medical results that

---

[8]It is possible to carry this point too far. After hearing a presentation on how physicists acknowledge that the nature of the universe is ultimately uncertain, a friend of one of the authors observed, "When those folks want to blow something up, they seem mighty certain about how do it!"

are inexplicable by science. That these results may be attributable to forces beyond human comprehension can be doubted by anyone, but it cannot be denied in the name of science. Nor should claims based on faith be used to justify intolerance of what science has to offer.

To bring the point closer to social science, consider the uses and limits of the science of psychoanalysis. We know that certain patterns of injurious behavior in adults can be traced to traumas suffered at an early age, but this does not mean that all behavior originates in childhood experiences. There are clearly other forces at work. Sigmund Freud, the founder of modern psychoanalysis, once remarked that about a third of his patients get better, a third stayed the same, and a third got worse. Not altogether bad, since he may have improved the odds for the first third; but this is nowhere close to the kind of result that a therapy based on perfect understanding would produce.

Consequently, psychoanalysis may be useful to some people in solving their problems, but it isn't an excuse for denying the possibility that there are alternative explanations for behavior—not until the evidence is much more precise. And even then, in this most human use of science, our very limitations as observers cannot lead to a claim of certainty for psychoanalysis—or any other science. Even the physical sciences operate in a cosmos surrounded by an infinity that defies measurement.

The message here is that a moral concern for humane values requires that there be a limit to both the arrogance of science as well as the claims of faith, intuition, and custom. If we are to deal with uncertainty effectively, a margin of tolerance for alternative forms of understanding is essential. Without it, we are likely to transcend the boundaries set by our human qualities. The results can be dangerous, as any number of religious executions, political massacres, and "scientifically justified" abuses of people's lives will testify.

Science is not a moral system. It is a strategy for learning about life and the universe—that and no more. Establishing the limits of faith, intuition, and custom is beyond the scope of this book, though our inquiry does suggest that all forms of knowledge should attempt to cohabit in the interests of civilized living. Apart from understanding where science leaves off and faith begins, it is important to be aware that there are other approaches to knowledge besides science and religion. Science confines itself to the observable and to what we have termed "reality testing." In this respect social scientists follow natural scientists, who build up generalizations about observable evidence. Yet the behavior of human beings differs from plants and rocks in that it may be driven by nonobservable forces and designs.

As an example, the ancient Greek philosopher Plato thought that what we see as "reality" is merely appearance—an appearance that is in the process of moving toward, or away from, some perfect ideal that is hidden from view. Thus, every particular chair that we see is but an imperfect realization of an ideal chair that exists only in human imagination. Similarly, any existing form of government is an approximation to an ideal form of government that can be derived from an understanding of the human condition. This changes the meaning of knowledge. In Plato's view, to "know" about the government of, say, Chicago is to see where it fits in relation to an ideal typology of governments. By comparison with this typology, the successes and failures of Chicago's government can be defined, and predictions can be made about its future performance.

As another example, Karl Marx confuses most scientifically oriented readers by seeming to offer many definitions for such key concepts as class, alienation, and exploitation. Yet all his definitions fit within a dynamic model of species struggling through various forms of historical development to realize its inner nature.

What is the inner nature of the human species? Marx approaches this question by distinguishing human beings from animals. What we have that they don't is the ability to choose what we produce. Animals produce hives and nests, for example, but they do it either by instinct or by accidental trial and error. Human beings, on the other hand, can take some twigs and make a nest, a boat, or some toothpicks. Marx believes that our species will become truly human when everyone spends a minimum of time producing for necessity, and a maximum of time in consciously chosen productive activity.

For Marx, then, exploitation is defined by the different ways that classes of people have used each other in various historical periods to secure necessities and achieve a measure of independence. The end of exploitation is a society in which all individuals will share the burden of necessary production so that all may share in the freedom of consciously chosen productive activity. It is to be a society in which there are no classes, no alienation, and no domination.

The forms of knowledge Plato and Marx developed are, in one sense, beyond the realm of science, since they rely on "essences" and "intrinsic relations" that cannot be observed directly. In another sense, the observable aspects of the predictions that Plato's system allows, or of the historical patterns that Marx identifies, can be examined by using scientific approaches that may shed light on their usefulness as explanations of what is observed.

It is also possible to enter the methodological world of Plato or Marx and challenge the fundamental assumptions about these essences and relations—or the adequacy and completeness of Marx's view of our "species-nature."[9] The point is that human beings have the capacity to think beyond what *is* to what *might be* or even to what *ought to be*. Prudence tells us that we need the best of all worlds of knowledge, not just the perfection of one of them.

Of Scientists, Science, and Paradigms

Science is practiced by people, not machines. Or, more accurately, science is practiced by groups of people. The major fields of social scientific inquiry are dominated by communities of

---

[9]For further exploration of these ideas, see Kenneth Hoover, *Ideology and Political Life*, 3rd ed. (New York: Harcourt, 2001), ch. 6. cf. Bertell Ollman, *Alienation: Marx's Theory of Human Nature*, 2nd ed. (New York: Cambridge University Press, 1976): Paul Thomas, "Marx and Science," *Political Studies* 24, no. 1 (1978): 1–23; Terence Ball and James Farr, eds., *After Marx* (Cambridge, England: Cambridge University Press, 1984), pp. 217–260; and James Farr, " Marx's Laws," *Political Studies* 34, no. 2 (1986): 202–222.

scientists, usually located at major research institutions, and tied together by a network of journals, conferences, and procedures for mutual evaluation and discussion.[10] Although substantial disagreements often exist within these **scientific communities,** there is usually a rough consensus about the boundaries of the principal problems, the standards for dealing with them, and the values that must inform the recommendations. No one in the American social scientific community, for example, writes about the desirability of dictatorial government.

The fact that there are communities of people involved in the enterprise of social science introduces a number of considerations that need to be reckoned with in evaluating social scientific research. First of all, few of us really like being unique or different from everyone else. Nor do people particularly enjoy having to face large problems from a point of view entirely their own. By this we mean that there is a natural psychological pressure toward **conformity** in all human activity, as well as in scientific inquiry.

Several factors reinforce this tendency toward conformity. One such factor is the **career structure** of academic disciplines. Though invisible to most students, careers in academic institutions typically hinge on a kind of master-apprentice system. Those who study with the famous master receive the best positions and the greatest access to means of communicating their views. Ability assuredly has a great deal to do with who gets close to the master and how successfully he or she manages to develop this position into a reputable scholarly career. But the net effect of this system is a significant pressure for the perpetuation of established viewpoints, since the apprentice frequently identifies with the position of his or her master.

To this pressure for conformity add yet another factor: the political significance of social scientific research. Researchers who probe elements of corruption in the economic system or in social welfare agencies, for example, are not likely to enjoy the

---

[10]An intriguing discussion of the history of science that details the role of scientific communities in structuring understanding is Thomas Kuhn's *The Structure of Scientific Revolutions,* 2nd ed. (Chicago: University of Chicago Press, 1970), on which some of these themes are based.

favor of their targets. Even the investigation of socioeconomic power as it enters into community decision making quickly becomes controversial. Since schools and institutions are usually run by trustees who represent dominant interests, there can be career risks in certain kinds of research projects.

Another factor influencing conformity with safer forms of social explanation is that research costs money. Survey research, upon which much good social science depends, costs a lot of money and usually requires financing from governmental agencies, businesses, or foundations. The kind of professional who attracts this money is not likely to be too far out of touch with prevailing social and political ideas.

For these reasons, scientific inquiry is frequently characterized by schools of thought or paradigms that structure the way in which problems are defined and solved. Yet in the face of all these pressures, the ultimate virtue of the scientific method, as opposed to other forms of inquiry, is that the steps by which knowledge is gathered are public and open to inspection and challenge. The point of reciting the factors that prejudice inquiry is not to discredit science, since most of these factors operate in other forms of inquiry as well, but rather to emphasize yet another reason for being critical of accepted knowledge and for being scientific in your own standards of evaluation. One of the first questions to ask when reading any book, taking any course, or selecting any field of research should be: What is the dominant paradigm behind this form of inquiry? Once that paradigm is understood, you are in a position to evaluate evidence carefully.

Making Social Science
Serve Human Needs

For all its usefulness as a tool of inquiry, social science, as we have seen, also carries within its methodology a potential for domination and manipulation. Typically, the researcher uses data about human behavior to answer the questions of the researcher, rather than those that the subject of the experiment may need to have answered. The design of the inquiry may turn the subject into a passive respondent, whose behavior is being interpreted or redefined in a manner that is out of the subject's control. Finally, the purposes for which the research is used may rest on the priorities of those who have power over others, whether or not that power is being used for legitimate ends in the service of human needs.

An interesting approach to these problems, and to some of the limitations of social scientific methodology we have described here, has been developed by William Foote Whyte, Davydd Greenwood, Peter Lazes, and their associates at Cornell University.[11] Termed **participatory action research**, this technique retains the spirit of social scientific inquiry while opening up the process in ways that expand its usefulness to people and generate creative solutions to problems. Two examples illustrate how the technique can be used.

The Xerox Corporation, inventor of modern copiers, was for a time threatened by a drastic loss of market share due to Japanese competition. The initial corporate response was to consider reducing labor costs by moving production jobs to nonunion areas. The focus of their analysis was on labor cost as the key variable, and the solution was simple: cut jobs and reduce wages. One researcher, called in to assist with this problem, suggested that the larger issue was the overall cost of production, not just direct labor, which accounted for less than 20 percent of the production cost, and that the workers themselves might have a few ideas about how to address it. By forming a "cost study team" with participation by researchers, union members, and management, the company identified a wide range of options. One of the more dramatic of these involved changing the ratio of indirect (nonproduction) employees to direct production workers from 2.1 to 1 in 1979 to 0.4 to 1 in 1985, while doubling total output. This was accomplished principally by shifting supervision and control functions to the workers themselves, while changing union rules to provide greater continuity of employment in various specializations.[12]

---

[11]Reported in William Foote Whyte, Davydd J. Greenwood, and Peter Lazes, "Participatory Action Research: Through Practice to Science in Social Research," *American Behavioral Scientists* 32, no. 5 (1989): 513–551.

[12]Whyte et al., "Participatory Action Research," pp. 524–525.

What is interesting from a methodological point of view is that the involvement of the "subjects" of the inquiry changed the definition of the key variables and the range of independent variables under consideration. Rather than just focusing on wage rates paid to production workers, the cost study team looked at training, continuity of the workforce, and the role of indirect employees. The result was that the needed savings were realized, and competitive pricing was restored.

A second illustration adds new dimensions to the discussion. William Foote Whyte and Kathleen Whyte became interested in a network of more than one hundred industrial cooperatives centered on the town of Mondragón in northern Spain.[13] These cooperatives included one of Spain's largest appliance manufacturers, as well as makers of electronic components and a wide array of internationally competitive products. The Mondragón network of producer cooperatives had established its own banking system, research institute, and health care and educational systems. The Mondragón cooperatives had achieved international significance as a model of worker ownership and control at a highly sophisticated level of production.

One classic problem faced by cooperatives is reconciling productive efficiency with significant levels of worker/owner participation. The question was how to analyze this problem so as to both enable Mondragón to succeed and allow for a kind of learning that would be transferable to other cooperative initiatives. A standard social scientific approach to measure participation would involve surveys of opinion about participation, together with analyses of instances of shared decision making. Based on these observations, generalizations could be developed about successful forms of participation.

---

[13]See their *Making Mondragón: The Growth and Dynamics of the Worker Cooperative Complex*, 2nd ed. (Ithaca, N.Y.: Cornell University ILR Press, 1991). Cf. Kenneth Hoover, review of *Making Mondragón* in *American Political Science Review* 84, no. 1 (1990): 351–352; and "Mondragón's Answers to Utopia's Problems," *Utopian Studies*, 3, no.2 (1992): 1–20.

The Whytes and their colleagues used this sort of research, but they put it together with a process of consultation and discussion that involved roundtables of cooperative worker/owners from various levels of the organization. Because the roundtables were asked not just to report on participation but to suggest ways of improving participation, previously unsuspected dimensions of participation were revealed and new variables could be conceptualized and measured. The "subjects" of the study became participants in the design of the research.

These researchers were led to realize all the more forcefully that ". . . measurement is driven by definitions. Poor definitions generate misleading measurements, which, added together, yield misleading conclusions."[14] By broadening the sources as well as the purposes of definitions, these researchers gained new insight into worker participation, in one case, and corporate management in another. In the Xerox example, they came to realize that what was at issue was far more than *worker productivity*; the question was *organizational performance* in a complex international environment. By working toward continuity of employment and increasing worker involvement in decision making, the overall performance of Xerox as a competitor was improved.

Note that the focus is on analysis directed toward *action* rather than just abstract understanding. This sort of inquiry is often referred to as *applied research*, which is thought to be the poorer cousin of *pure research*—meaning research devoted solely to intellectual questions. The point here is that in these cases, research applied to action yielded conceptualizations and results that a "pure" researcher might never have obtained. As the authors of this approach point out:

> Rethinking past practice leads to theoretical reformulation that in turn leads to improved practice. The processes of rethinking both theory and practice thus strengthen both theory and practice.[15]

---

[14]Whyte et al., "Participatory Action Research," p. 548.
[15]Ibid., p. 540.

Participatory action research has the effect of bringing into play all three levels of analysis discussed earlier in this chapter: *factuality, reality,* and *actuality.* The result in both cases is that this form of research has now been incorporated into the organizations themselves as a means of adapting to changing circumstances.

It may be a while before you are called in by Xerox to reorganize the company or asked to travel to Spain to investigate cooperatives; but this style of research has useful applications, whether you are studying participation in student elections, the responses of people to political advertising, or the sense of class and status that people live with in the workplace.

The Radicalism of Science

After what has been said about the conformist tendencies of the scientific establishment, even allowing for a brief message of reconsideration at the end, it may seem perverse to start talking about **scientific radicalism.** So be it; not all has yet been said on the subject. Science can be radical in a social sense and a personal sense as well.

Scientific inquiry began as a revolt against dogma established and controlled by dominant political and social institutions. The history of science contains some important cases of intrepid analysts who emerged from their laboratories with findings that threatened prevailing understandings in various fields of human inquiry. Some scientists have paid even with their lives for such heresies. After all, the control of information is one of the fundamentals of political power. Scientists who insist on open and accountable procedures of information gathering and conclusion formation chip away at the power of those who would foreclose inquiry in favor of pet theories and self-serving ideologies and doctrines.

More relevant to daily life are the ways in which a scientific habit of mind can contribute to your own ability to resist conditioning and to deal knowledgeably with your environment. We are all bombarded with arguments to do this or that based on somebody else's conception of what is good and bad. For most people most of the time, estimations of the credibility of sources suffice to separate the smart advice from the nonsense. But it doesn't hurt to have a means of independent evaluation.

Western culture has for a long time viewed social problems as a matter of weakness of human nature. This approach invites introspection and the examination of personal intentions, motives, and dispositions. Social science, by and large, encourages a different approach: Look around you. Before deciding that the individual is totally responsible for his or her actions, consider the environmental factors, the structures of power, the forces of conditioning, the real dimensions of choice that face people in social situations, and the material possibilities people actually have of solving their own problems. These circumstances are sometimes more susceptible to change than are inward dispositions that grow out of heredity as well as a conscious and unconscious history of individual development.

Science enters into personal action as a method for disciplining the process of understanding experience. The safeguards of the scientific method exist principally to control the natural tendency to project on what is observed whatever we want the world to be for our own private purposes. A discipline it is, but it becomes in practice a method of personal liberation from the narrowness of our own views, the limits of our own powers of observation, and the pressures of our prejudices. Science, a discipline all may develop, can become a radical force in a world that badly needs to be changed.

Science and Politics

There is no shortage of well-meant ideas for improving society. What is more often missing is a good method. Imposing utopia through the state, as Marxist-Leninists tried to do, or leaving its arrival to the voluntary action of self-interested individuals carries great hazards. Basic human rights are the first casualty of the statist method, and the loss of community values is frequently the result of the second. Well-informed and disciplined understanding can help avoid the worst excesses of both methods and establish the basis for interpersonal agreement without the use of coercion or the selfish assertion of one interest over another. A trenchant observer of politics reminds us:

> If political developments depended upon factual observations, false meanings would be discredited in time and a consensus upon valid ones would emerge, at least among informed and educated observers. That does not happen, even over long time periods. The characteristic of problems, leaders, and enemies that makes them political is precisely that controversy over their meanings is not resolved. . . . There is no politics respecting matters that evoke a consensus about the pertinent facts, their meanings, and the rational course of action.[16]

Without conceding all that may be implied in this critique of politics, the statement can be turned around. *To the extent that social issues can be dealt with on the basis of reliable information, the potential for conflict resolution is much higher.* Methodological discipline is a means of minimizing the distortion of information while maximizing the opportunities for mutual understanding.

There remain, of course, those essentially contestable issues over which agreement is much harder to reach, if not impossible.[17] Citizens and political leaders, unlike most scientists, are faced with the necessity for action. In the most constructive uses of politics, people achieve new insights and find shared interests that yield effective forms of community action. The methods described in this book, practiced in a democratic context, can

---

[16]Murray Edelman, *Constructing the Political Spectacle* (Chicago: University of Chicago Press, 1998), pp. 2–3.

[17]For an interesting exploration of "essentially contestable concepts" and their meaning for politics, see William Connolly, *The Terms of Political Discourse*, 2nd ed. (Princeton, N.J.: Priceton University Press, 1983).

help that to happen, as they did in the Xerox and Mondragón examples. The realm of politics can include the honest search for truth by social scientific methods and other strategies as well, even though some differences must ultimately be resolved through political decision-making processes.

There is another potential in politics. It relies on the orchestration of meaning through symbolic appeals, and on the skillful use of threats and reassurances to mobilize support and induce quiescence among the possible opposition.[18] At the core of this kind of politics is the manipulation of information and, with it, of people. On the other hand, science deals with information in ways that can improve politics. A much-respected teacher once observed that "science is a way of organizing evidence—one that requires a social process of decision making that guards against rule by the few, as well as rule by the ignorant."[19]

Science and politics are both about the resolution of uncertainties, and both involve the demonstration of the truth. It was, after all, Mahatma Gandhi who brought down British colonial rule in India by a political technique he called *truth-force (satyagraha)*. Gandhi organized protests that made clear the exploitative nature of British colonial rule. The British, once exposed to the pressure of world public opinion as well as to the concerted action of a newly mobilized populace, were forced to acquiesce.[20] The leaders of the American civil rights movement, many of whom studied Gandhi's technique, did the same in confronting legal segregation in the United States.[21] The truth of exploitation

[18]For examples, see Edelman, *Constructing the Political Spectacle*, chs. 3–5.

[19]The reference is to Aage Clausen, who has given invaluable advice in the writing of this book.

[20]For an analysis of the dynamics of *truth-forces*, see Erik Erikson, *Gandhi's Truth* (New York: Norton, 1969). The discussion of *factuality, reality,* and *actuality* earlier in the chapter was drawn from Erikson's examination of Gandhi's technique. See especially p. 396. Cf. Robert Coles, *Erik H. Erikson. The Growth of His Work* (New York; Norton, 1970), pp. 267–399.

[21]Steven Oates, in his biography *Let the Trumpet Sound: The Life of Martin Luther King, Jr.* (New York: Harper & Row, 1982), reviews the development of King's approach to political leadership.

and domination, once made clear through analysis and demonstration, turns out to be more powerful than manipulation, deceit, and coercion itself.

Ultimately, both *truth-force* and social scientific methodology depend on a moral commitment to the values of honesty and integrity. The attempt to confront error and misunderstanding, to be credible, must rest on the search for truth. Without such a commitment, political action is dangerous and science is a fraud.

• CONCEPTS INTRODUCED

Factuality   Conformist social explanation
Reality   Career structures
Actuality   Participatory action research
Observational studies   Scientific radicalism
Scientific communities

APPENDIX A

TUNING IN, TUNING OUT:
THE STRANGE DISAPPEARANCE
OF SOCIAL CAPITAL IN AMERICA

ROBERT D. PUTNAM
Harvard University

. . . For the last year or so, I have been wrestling with a difficult mystery. It is, if I am right, a puzzle of some importance to the future of American democracy. It is a classic brain-teaser, with a corpus delicti, a crime scene strewn with clues, and many potential suspects. As in all good detective stories, however, some plausible miscreants turn out to have impeccable alibis, and some important clues hint at portentous developments that occurred long before the curtain rose. Moreover, like Agatha Christie's *Murder on the Orient Express*, this crime may have had more than one perpetrator, so that we shall need to sort out ringleaders from accomplices. Finally, I need to make clear at the outset that I am not yet sure that I have solved the mystery. In that sense, this represents work-in-progress. I have a prime suspect that I am prepared to indict, but the evidence is not yet strong enough to convict, so I invite your help in sifting clues.

© Edited excerpt from "Tuning In, Tuning Out: The Strange Disappearance of Social Capital in the United States," the 1995 Ithiel de Sola Pool Lecture, *PS: Political Science and Politics,* pp. 664–682. Reprinted with permission of Cambridge University Press.

Theories and Measures of Social Capital

Several years ago I conducted research on the arcane topic of local government in Italy (Putnam 1993). That study concluded that the performance of government and other social institutions is powerfully influenced by citizen engagement in community affairs, or what (following Coleman 1990) I termed *social capital*. I am now seeking to apply that set of ideas and insights to the urgent problems of contemporary American public life.

By *social capital*, I mean features of social life—networks, norms, and trust—that enable participants to act together more effectively to pursue shared objectives. Whether or not their shared goals are praiseworthy is, of course, entirely another matter. To the extent that the norms, networks, and trust link substantial sectors of the community and span underlying social cleavages—to the extent that the social capital is of a "bridging" sort—then the enhanced cooperation is likely to serve broader interests and to be widely welcomed. . . .

Social capital, in short, refers to social connections and the attendant norms and trust. Who benefits from these connections, norms, and trust—the individual, the wider community, or some faction within the community—must be determined empirically, not definitionally.[1] . . . For present purposes, I am concerned with forms of social capital that, generally speaking, serve civic ends.

Social capital in this sense is closely related to political participation in the conventional sense, but these terms are not synonymous. Political participation refers to our relations with political institutions. Social capital refers to our relations with one another. Sending a check to a PAC is an act of political participation, but it does not embody or create social capital. Bowling in a league or having coffee with a friend embodies and creates social capital, though these are not acts of political participation. (A grassroots political movement or a traditional

---

[1]In this respect I deviate slightly from James Coleman's "functional" definition of social capital. See Coleman (1990): 300–21.

urban machine is a social capital-intensive form of political participation.) I use the term "civic engagement" to refer to people's connections with the life of their communities, not merely with politics. Civic engagement is correlated with political participation in a narrower sense, but whether they move in lockstep is an empirical question, not a logical certitude. Some forms of individualized political participation, such as check-writing, for example, might be rising at the same time that social connectedness was on the wane. Similarly, although social trust—trust in other people—and political trust— trust in political authorities—might be empirically related, they are logically quite distinct. I might well trust my neighbors without trusting city hall, or vice versa.

The theory of social capital presumes that, generally speaking, the more we connect with other people, the more we trust them, and vice versa. At least in the contexts I have so far explored, this presumption generally turns out to be true: social trust and civic engagement are strongly correlated. That is, with or without controls for education, age, income, race, gender, and so on, people who join are people who trust.[2] Moreover, this is true across different countries, and across different states in the United States, as well as across individuals, and it is true of all sorts of groups.[3] Sorting out which way causation flows—whether joining causes trusting or trusting causes joining—is complicated both theoretically and methodologically, although John Brehm and Wendy Rahn (1995) report evidence that the causation flows mainly from joining to trusting. Be that as it may, civic connections and social trust move together. Which way are they moving?

[2]The results reported in this paragraph and throughout the paper, unless otherwise indicated, are derived from the General Social Survey.

[3]Across the 35 countries for which data are available from the World Values Survey (1990–91), the correlation between the average number of associational memberships and endorsement of the view that "most people can be trusted" is r .65.

***Bowling Alone: Trends
in Civic Engagement***

Evidence from a number of independent sources strongly suggests that America's stock of social capital has been shrinking for more than a quarter century.

- Membership records of such diverse organizations as the PTA, the Elks club, the League of Women Voters, the Red Cross, labor unions, and even bowling leagues show that participation in many conventional voluntary associations has declined by roughly 25% to 50% over the last two to three decades (Putnam 1995, 1996).
- Surveys of the time budgets of average Americans in 1965, 1975, and 1985, in which national samples of men and women recorded every single activity undertaken during the course of a day, imply that the time we spend on informal socializing and visiting is down (perhaps by one quarter) since 1965, and that the time we devote to clubs and organizations is down even more sharply (probably by roughly half) over this period.
- While Americans' interest in politics has been stable or even growing over the last three decades, and some forms of participation that require moving a pen, such as signing petitions and writing checks, have increased significantly, many measures of collective participation have fallen sharply (Rosenstone and Hansen 1993; Putnam 1996), including attending a rally or speech (off 36% between 1973 and 1993), attending a meeting on town or school affairs (off 39%), or working for a political party (off 56%).
- Evidence from the General Social Survey demonstrates, at all levels of education and among both men and women, a drop of roughly one-quarter in group membership since 1974 and a drop of roughly one-third in social trust since 1972.[4] . . . Slumping membership has afflicted all sorts of groups, from sports clubs and professional associations to literary discussion groups and labor

[4]Trust in political authorities—and indeed in many social institutions—has also declined sharply over the last three decades, but that is conceptually a distinct trend. As we shall see later, the etiology of the slump in social trust is quite different from the etiology of the decline in political trust.

unions.⁵ . . . Furthermore, Gallup polls report that church attendance fell by roughly 15% during the 1960s and has remained at that lower level ever since, while data from the National Opinion Research Center suggest that the decline continued during the 1970s and 1980s and by now amounts to roughly 30% (Putnam 1996).

. . .

A fuller audit of American social capital would need to account for apparent counter-trends. Some observers believe, for example, that support groups and neighborhood watch groups are proliferating, and few deny that the last several decades have witnessed explosive growth in interest groups represented in Washington. . . . However, these are not really associations in which members meet one another. Their members' ties are to common symbols and ideologies, but not to each other. . . . With due regard to various kinds of counter-evidence, I believe that the weight of the available evidence confirms that Americans today are significantly less engaged with their communities than was true a generation ago.

Of course, lots of civic activity is still visible in our communities. American civil society is not moribund. Indeed, evidence suggests that America still outranks many other countries in the degree of our community involvement and social trust (Putnam 1996). But if we compare ourselves, not with other countries but with our parents, the best available evidence suggests that we are less connected with one another.

This prologue poses a number of important questions that merit further debate:

- Is it true that America's stock of social capital has diminished?
- Does it matter?
- What can we do about it?

The answer to the first two questions is, I believe, "yes," but I cannot address them further in this setting. Answering the third

⁵For reasons explained below, Figure 1 reports trends for membership in various types of groups *controlling for* the respondent's education level.

question—which ultimately concerns me most—depends, at least in part, on first understanding the *causes* of the strange malady afflicting American civic life. This is the mystery I seek to unravel here: Why, beginning in the 1960s and accelerating in the 1970s and 1980s, did the fabric of American community life begin to fray? Why are more Americans bowling alone?

Explaining the Erosion of Social Capital

Many possible answers have been suggested for this puzzle:

- Busyness and time pressure
- Economic hard times (or, according to alternative theories, material affluence)
- Residential mobility
- Suburbanization
- The movement of women into the paid labor force and the stresses of two-career families
- Disruption of marriage and family ties
- Changes in the structure of the American economy, such as the rise of chain stores, branch firms, and the service sector
- The Sixties (most of which actually happened in the Seventies), including

  —Vietnam, Watergate, and disillusion with public life
  —The cultural revolt against authority (sex, drugs, and so on)

- Growth of the welfare state
- The civil rights revolution
- Television, the electronic revolution, and other technological changes

Most respectable mystery writers would hesitate to tally up this many plausible suspects, no matter how energetic the fictional detective. I am not yet in a position to address all these theories—certainly not in any definitive form—but we must begin to winnow the list. To be sure, a social trend as pervasive as the one we are investigating probably has multiple causes, so our task is to assess the relative importance of such factors as these.

A solution, even a partial one, to our mystery must pass several tests.

Is the proposed explanatory factor correlated with trust and civic engagement? If not, it is difficult to see why that factor should even be placed in the lineup. For example, many women have entered the paid labor force during the period in question, but if working women turned out to be more engaged in community life than housewives, it would be harder to attribute the downturn in community organizations to the rise of two-career families.

Is the correlation spurious? If parents, for example, were more likely to be joiners than childless people, that might be an important clue. However, if the correlation between parental status and civic engagement turned out to be entirely spurious, due to the effects of (say) age, we would have to remove the declining birth rate from our list of suspects.

Is the proposed explanatory factor changing in the relevant way? Suppose, for instance, that people who often move have shallower community roots. That could be an important part of the answer to our mystery *only if* residential mobility itself had risen during this period.

Is the proposed explanatory factor vulnerable to the claim that it might be the result *of civic disengagement, not the cause?* For example, even if newspaper readership were closely correlated with civic engagement across individuals and across time, we would need to weigh the possibility that reduced newspaper circulation is the result (not the cause) of disengagement.

Against that set of benchmarks, let us consider various potential influences on social capital formation.

Education

Human capital and social capital are closely related, for education has a very powerful effect on trust and associational membership, as well as many other forms of social and political participation. Education is by far the strongest correlate that I have discovered of civic engagement in all its forms, including social trust and membership in many different types of groups.[6] . . . Education, in short, is an extremely powerful predictor of civic engagement. . . .

Education is in part a proxy for social class and economic differences, but when income, social status, and education are used together to predict trust and group membership, education continues to be the primary influence. . . . In short, highly educated people are much more likely to be joiners and trusters, partly because they are better off economically, but mostly because of the skills, resources, and inclinations that were imparted to them at home and in school.

It is widely recognized that Americans today are better educated than our parents and grandparents. It is less often appreciated how massively and rapidly this trend has transformed the educational composition of the adult population during just the last two decades. Since 1972, the proportion of all adults with . . . more than 12 years has nearly doubled, rising from 28% to 50%. . . .

Thus, education boosts civic engagement sharply, and educational levels have risen massively. Unfortunately, these two undeniable facts only deepen our central mystery. By itself, the rise in educational levels should have *increased* social capital during the last 20 years. . . . By contrast, however, the actual GSS figures show a net *decline* since the early 1970s. . . .

Thus, this first investigative foray leaves us more mystified than before. We may nevertheless draw two useful conclusions from these findings, one methodological and one substantive:

1. Since education has such a powerful effect on civic engagement and social trust, we need to take account of educational differences in our exploration of other possible factors, in order to be sure that we do not confuse the consequences of education with the possible effects of other variables.
2. Whatever forces lie behind the slump in civic engagement and social trust, those forces have affected all levels in American society. The mysterious disengagement of the last quarter

---

[6]The only exceptions are farm groups, labor unions, and veterans' organizations, whose members have slightly less formal education than the average American.

century seems to have afflicted all echelons of our society. . . . The mysterious disengagement of the last quarter century seems to have afflicted all echelons of our society.

Pressures of Time and Money

Americans certainly *feel* busier now than a generation ago: the proportion of us who report feeling "always rushed" jumped by half between the mid-1960s and the mid-1990s (Robinson and Godbey 1995). Probably the most obvious suspect behind our tendency to drop out of community affairs is pervasive busyness. And lurking nearby in the shadows are those endemic economic pressures so much discussed nowadays—job insecurity and declining real wages, especially among the lower two-thirds of the income distribution.

Yet, however culpable busyness and economic insecurity may appear at first glance, it is hard to find any incriminating evidence. In fact, the balance of the evidence argues that pressures of time and money are apparently *not* important contributors to the puzzle we seek to solve.

In the first place, time budget studies do *not* confirm the thesis that Americans are, on average, working longer than a generation ago. On the contrary, Robinson and Godbey (1995) report a five-hour per week *gain* in free time for the average American between 1965 and 1985, due partly to reduced time spent on housework and partly to earlier retirement. Their claim that Americans have more leisure time now than several decades ago is, to be sure, contested by other observers. Schor (1991), for example, reports evidence that our work hours are lengthening, especially for women. Whatever the resolution of that controversy, however, the thesis that attributes civic disengagement to longer workdays is rendered much less plausible by looking at the correlation between work hours, on the one hand, and social trust and group membership, on the other.

The available evidence strongly suggests that, in fact, long hours on the job are *not* associated with lessened involvement in civic life or reduced social trust. Quite the reverse: Results from the General Social Survey show that employed people belong to somewhat *more* groups than those outside the paid labor force. Even more striking is the fact that among workers, longer hours are linked to *more* civic engagement, not less.[7] This surprising discovery is fully consistent with evidence from the time budget studies. Robinson (1990a) reports that, unsurprisingly, people who spend more time at work do feel more rushed, and these harried souls do spend less time eating, sleeping, reading books, engaging in hobbies, and just doing nothing. Compared to the rest of the population, they also spend a lot less time watching television—almost 30% less. However, they do *not* spend less time on organizational activity. . . .

. . . Moreover, the nationwide falloff in joining and trusting is perfectly mirrored among full-time workers, among part-time workers, and among those outside the paid labor force. So if people are dropping out of community life, long hours do not seem to be the reason.

If time pressure is not the culprit we seek, how about financial pressures? . . . The declines in engagement and trust are actually somewhat greater among the more affluent segments of the American public than among the poor and middle-income wage-earners. . . . In short, neither objective nor subjective economic well-being has inoculated Americans against the virus of civic disengagement; if anything, affluence has slightly exacerbated the problem. . . .

[7]This is true with or without controls for education and year of survey. The patterns among men and women on this score are not identical, for women who work part-time appear to be somewhat more civically engaged and socially trusting than either those who work full-time or those who do not work outside the home at all. Whatever we make of this intriguing anomaly, which apparently does not appear in the time budget data (Robinson and Godbey 1995) and which has no counterpart in the male half of the population, it cannot account for our basic puzzle, since female part-time workers constitute a relatively small fraction of the American population, and the fraction is growing, not declining. Between the first half of the 1970s and the first half of the 1990s, according to the GSS data, the fraction of the total adult population constituted by female part-time workers rose from about 8% to about 10%.

Mobility and Suburbanization

Many studies have found that residential stability and such related phenomena as homeownership are associated with greater civic engagement. At an earlier stage in this investigation (Putnam 1995, 30), I observed that "mobility, like frequent repotting of plants, tends to disrupt root systems, and it takes time for an uprooted individual to put down new roots." I must now report, however, that further inquiry fully exonerates residential mobility from any responsibility for our fading civic engagement. Data from the U.S. Bureau of the Census 1995 (and earlier years) show that rates of residential mobility have been remarkably constant over the last half century. In fact, to the extent that there has been any change at all, both long-distance and short-distance mobility have *declined* over the last five decades. During the 1950s, 20% of Americans changed residence each year and 6.9% annually moved across county borders; during the 1990s, the comparable figures are 17% and 6.6%. Americans, in short, are today slightly *more* rooted residentially than a generation ago. If the verdict on the economic distress interpretation had to be nuanced, the verdict on mobility is unequivocal. This theory is simply wrong.

But if moving itself has not eroded our social capital, what about the possibility that we have moved to places—especially the suburbs—that are less congenial to social connectedness? To test this theory, we must first examine the correlation between place of residence and social capital. In fact, social connectedness does differ by community type, but the differences turn out to be modest and in directions that are inconsistent with the theory. . . .

The Changing Role of Women

Most of (my generation's) mothers were housewives, and most of them invested heavily in social capital formation—a jargony way of referring to untold, unpaid hours in church suppers, PTA meetings, neighborhood coffee klatches, and visits to friends and relatives. The movement of women out of the home and into the paid labor force is probably the most portentous social change of the last half century. However welcome and overdue the feminist revolution may be, it is hard to believe that it has had no impact on social connectedness. Could this be the primary reason for the decline of social capital over the last generation?

Some patterns in the available survey evidence seem to support this claim. All things considered, women belong to somewhat fewer voluntary associations than men (Edwards, Edwards, and Watts 1984). On the other hand, time budget studies suggest that women spend more time on those groups and more time in informal social connecting than men (Robinson and Godbey 1995). Although the absolute declines in joining and trusting are approximately equivalent among men and women, the relative declines are somewhat greater among women. Controlling for education, memberships among men have declined at a rate of about 10–15% a decade, compared to about 20–25% a decade for women. . . .

As we saw earlier, however, work status itself seems to have little net impact on group membership or on trust. Housewives belong to different types of groups than do working women (more PTAs, for example, and fewer professional associations), but in the aggregate working women are actually members of slightly more voluntary associations.[8] Moreover, the overall declines in civic engagement are somewhat greater among housewives than among employed women. Comparison of time budget data between 1965 and 1985 (Robinson and Godbey 1995) seems to show that employed women as a group are actually spending more time on organizations than before, while nonemployed women are spending less. This same study suggests that the major decline in informal socializing since 1965 has also been concentrated among non-employed women. The central fact, of course, is that the overall trends are down for all categories of

[8]Robinson and Godbey (1995), however, report that nonemployed women still spend more time on activity in voluntary associations than their employed counterparts.

women (and for men, too—even bachelors), but the figures suggest that women who work full-time actually may have been more
resistant to the slump than those who do not.

Thus, although women appear to have borne a dispropor-
tionate share of the decline in civic engagement over the last two
decades, it is not easy to find any micro-level data that tie that
fact directly to their entry into the labor force. It is hard to control for selection bias in these data, of course, because women
who have chosen to enter the workforce doubtless differ in many
respects from women who have chosen to stay home. Perhaps
one reason that community involvement appears to be rising
among working women and declining among working housewives
is that precisely the sort of women who, in an earlier era, were
most involved with their communities have been disproportion-
ately likely to enter the workforce, thus simultaneously lowering
the average level of civic engagement among the remaining
homemakers and raising the average among women in the workplace. Obviously, we have not been running a great national
controlled experiment on the effects of work on women's civic
engagement, and in any event the patterns in the data are not
entirely clear. Contrary to my own earlier speculations, however,
I can find little evidence to support the hypothesis that the movement of women into the workplace over the last generation has
played a major role in the reduction of social connectedness and
civic engagement. On the other hand, I have no clear alternative
explanation for the fact that the relative declines are greater
among women than men. Since this evidence is at best circumstantial, perhaps the best interim judgment here is the famous
Scots verdict: not proven.

Marriage and Family

Another widely discussed social trend that more or less coincides
with the downturn in civic engagement is the breakdown of the
traditional family unit—mom, dad, and the kids. Since
the family itself is, by some accounts, a key form of social capital,

perhaps its eclipse is part of the explanation for the reduction in joining and trusting in the wider community. What does the evidence show?

First of all, evidence of the loosening of family bonds is unequivocal. In addition to the century-long increase in divorce rates (which accelerated in the mid-1960s to the mid-1970s and then leveled off), and the more recent increase in single-parent families, the incidence of one-person households has more than doubled since 1950, in part because of the rising number of widows living alone (Caplow, Bahr, Modell, and Chadwick 1991, 47, 106, 113). The net effect of all these changes, as reflected in the General Social Survey, is that the proportion of all American adults who are currently unmarried climbed from 28% in 1974 to 48% in 1994.

Second, married men and women do rank somewhat higher on both our measures of social capital. That is, controlling for education, age, race, and so on, single people—both men and women, divorced, separated and never-married—are significantly less trusting and less engaged civically than married people.[9] Roughly speaking, married men and women are about a third more trusting and belong to about 15–25% more groups than comparable single men and women. (Widows and widowers are more like married people than single people in this comparison.)

In short, successful marriage (especially if the family unit includes children) is statistically associated with greater social trust and civic engagement. Thus, some part of the decline in both trust and membership is tied to the decline in marriage. . . .

My own verdict (based in part on additional evidence to be introduced later) is that the disintegration of marriage is probably an accessory to the crime, but not the major villain of the piece.

---

[9]Multivariate analysis hints that one major reason why divorce lowers connectedness is that it lowers family income, which in turn reduces civic engagement.

The Rise of the Welfare State

Circumstantial evidence, particularly the timing of the downturn in social connectedness, has suggested to some observers (for example, Fukuyama 1995, 313–314) that an important cause—perhaps even *the* cause—of civic disengagement is big government and the growth of the welfare state. By "crowding out" private initiative, it is argued, state intervention has subverted civil society. This is a much larger topic than I can address in detail here, but a word or two may be appropriate.

On the one hand, some government policies have almost certainly had the effect of destroying social capital. For example, the so-called "slum clearance" policies of the 1950s and 1960s replaced physical capital, by disrupting existing community ties. It is also conceivable that certain social expenditures and tax policies may have created disincentives for civic-minded philanthropy. On the other hand, it is much harder to see which government policies might be responsible for the decline in bowling leagues and literary clubs.

One empirical approach to this issue is to examine differences in civic engagement and public policy across different political jurisdictions to see whether swollen government leads to shriveled social capital. Among the U.S. states, however, differences in social capital appear essentially uncorrelated with various measures of welfare spending or government size.[10] . . .

[10]I have set aside this issue for fuller treatment in later work. However, I note for the record that (1) state-level differences in social trust and group membership are substantial, closely intercorrelated and reasonably stable, at least over the period from the 1970s to the 1990s, and (2) those differences are suprisingly closely correlated ($R^2 = .52$) with the measure of "state political culture" invented by Elazar (1966), and refined by Sharkansky (1969), based on descriptive accounts of state politics during the 1950s and traceable in turn to patterns of immigration during the nineteenth century and before.

Race and the Civil Rights Revolution

Race is such an absolutely fundamental feature of American social history that nearly every other feature of our society is connected to it in some way. Thus, it seems intuitively plausible that race might somehow have played a role in the erosion of social capital over the last generation. In fact, some observers (both black and white) have noted that the decline in social connectedness and social trust began just after the greatest successes of the civil rights revolution of the 1960s. To some, that coincidence has suggested the possibility of a kind of sociological "white flight," as legal desegregation of civic life led whites to withdraw from community associations.

Like the theory about the welfare state, this racial interpretation of the destruction of social capital is highly controversial and can hardly be settled within the compass of these brief remarks. Nevertheless, the basic facts are these.

First, racial differences in associational membership are not large. . . . On the other hand, racial differences in social trust are very large indeed, even taking into account differences in education, income, and so on. On average, during the 1972–94 period, controlling for educational differences, about 17% of blacks endorsed the view that "most people can be trusted," as compared to about 45% of whites, and about 27% of respondents of other races.[11] These racial differences in social trust, of course, reflect not collective paranoia, but real experiences over many generations.

Second, the erosion of social capital has affected all races. . . . Even more important, the pace of disengagement among whites has been uncorrelated with racial intolerance or support for segregation. Avowedly racist or segregationist whites have been no quicker to drop out of community organizations during this period than more tolerant whites. . . . This evidence also suggests that reversing the civil rights gains of the last 30 years would do nothing to reverse the social capital losses.

---

[11]As elsewhere in this essay, "controlling for educational differences" here means averaging the average scores for respondents with fewer than 12 years of schooling, with exactly 12 years, and with more than 12 years, respectively.

Generational Effects

Our efforts thus far to localize the sources of civic disengagement have been singularly unfruitful. The downtrends are uniform across the major categories of American society. . . . One notable exception to this uniformity, however, involves age. In all our statistical analyses, age is second only to education as a predictor of all forms of civic engagement and trust. Older people belong to more organizations than young people, and they are less misanthropic. Older Americans also vote more often and read newspapers more frequently, two other forms of civic engagement closely correlated with joining and trusting. . . . Most observers have interpreted this pattern as a life cycle phenomenon, and so, at first, did I.

Evidence from the General Social Survey (GSS) enables us to follow individual cohorts as they age. . . . Startlingly, however, such an analysis, repeated for successive birth cohorts, produces virtually no evidence of such life cycle changes in civic engagement. In fact, as various generations moved through the period between 1972 and 1994, their levels of trust and membership more often fell than rose, reflecting a more or less simultaneous decline in civic engagement among young and old alike, particularly during the second half of the 1980s. But that downtrend obviously cannot explain why, throughout the period, older Americans were always more trusting and engaged. In fact, the only reliable life cycle effect visible in these data is a withdrawal from civic engagement very late in life, as we move through our 80s.

The central paradox posed by these patterns is this: Older people are consistently more engaged and trusting than younger people, yet we do not become more engaged and trusting as we age. What's going on here?

Time and age are notoriously ambiguous in their effects on social behavior. Social scientists have learned to distinguish three contrasting phenomena:

1. *Life-cycle effects* represent differences attributable to stage of life. In this case individuals change as they age, but since effects of aging are, in the aggregate, neatly balanced by the

"demographic metabolism" of births and deaths, life cycle effects produce no aggregate change. Everyone's close-focus eyesight worsens as we age, but the aggregate demand for reading glasses changes little.

2. *Period effects* affect all people who live through a given era, regardless of their age.[12] Period effects can produce both individual and aggregate change, often quickly and enduringly, without any age-related differences. The sharp drop in trust in government between 1965 and 1975, for example, was almost entirely this sort of period effect, as Americans of all ages changed their minds about their leaders' trustworthiness. Similarly, as just noted, a modest portion of the decline in social capital during the 1980s appears to be a period effect.

3. *Generational effects*, as described in Karl Mannheim's classic essay on "The Problem of Generations," represent the fact that "[i]ndividuals who belong to the same generation, who share the same year of birth, are endowed, to that extent, with a common location in the historical dimension of the social process" (Mannheim 1952, 290). Like life cycle effects (and unlike typical period effects), generational effects show up as disparities among age groups at a single point in time, but like period effects (and unlike life cycle effects) generational effects produce real social change, as successive generations, enduringly "imprinted" with divergent outlooks, enter and leave the population. In pure generational effects, no individual ever changes, but society does.

. . . Returning to our conundrum, how could older people today be more engaged and trusting, if they did not become more engaged and trusting as they aged? The key to this paradox, as David Butler and Donald Stokes (1974) observed in another context, is to ask, not *how old people are*, but *when they were young*. Figure 1 addresses this reformulated question, displaying

---

[12]Period effects that affect only people of a specific age shade into generational effects, which is why Converse, when summarizing these age-related effects, refers to "two-and-a-half" types, rather than the conventional three types.

FIGURE 1 · SOCIAL CAPITAL AND CIVIC ENGAGEMENT BY GENERATION (EDUCATION CONTROLLED)

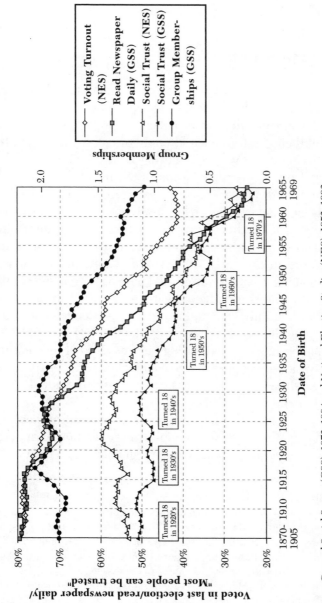

SOURCE: General Social Survey (GSS), 1972–1994 and National Election Studies (NES), 1952–1992
Respondents aged 25–80. Five-year moving average.
Equal weighting of three educational categories.

179

various measures of civic engagement according to the respondents' year of birth.[13] . . .

The Long Civic Generation

In effect, Figure 1 lines up Americans from left to right according to their date of birth, beginning with those born in the last third of the nineteenth century and continuing across to the generation of their great-grandchildren, born in the last third of the twentieth century. As we begin moving along this queue from left to right—from those raised around the turn of the century to those raised during the Roaring Twenties, and so on—we find relatively high and unevenly rising levels of civic engagement and social trust. Then rather abruptly, however, we encounter signs of reduced community involvement, starting with men and women born in the early 1930s. Remarkably, this downward trend in joining, trusting, voting, and newspaper reading continues almost uninterruptedly for nearly 40 years. The trajectories for the various different indicators of civic engagement are strikingly parallel: each shows a high, sometimes rising plateau for people born and raised during the first third of the century; each shows a turning point in the cohorts born around 1930; and each then shows a more or less constant decline down to the cohorts born during the 1960s.[14]

By any standard, these intergenerational differences are extraordinary. Compare, for example, the generation born in the early 1920s with the generation of their grandchildren born in the

[13]To exclude the life cycle effects in the last years of life, Figure 1 excludes respondents over 80. To avoid well-known problems in reliably sampling young adults, as discussed by Converse (1976), Figure 1 also excludes respondents aged under 25. To offset the relatively small year-by-year samples and to control for educational differences, Figure 1 charts five-year moving averages across the three educational categories used in this essay.

[14]I learned of the Miller/Shanks argument only after discovering generational differences in civic engagement in the General Social Survey data, but their findings and mine are strikingly consistent.

late 1960s. Controlling for educational disparities, members of the generation born in the 1920s belong to almost twice as many civic associations as those born in the late 1960s (roughly 1.9 memberships per capita, compared to roughly 1.1 memberships per capita). The grandparents are more than twice as likely to trust other people (50–60% compared with 25% for the grandchildren). They vote at nearly double the rate of the most recent cohorts (roughly 75% compared with 40–45%), and they read newspapers almost three times as often (70–80% read a paper daily compared with 25–30%). And bear in mind that we have found no evidence that the youngest generation will come to match their grandparent's higher levels of civic engagement as they grow older.

Thus, read not as life cycle effects, but rather as generational effects, the age-related patterns in our data suggest a radically different interpretation of our basic puzzle. Deciphered with this key, Figure 1 depicts a long "civic" generation, born roughly between 1910 and 1940, a broad group of people substantially more engaged in community affairs and substantially more trusting than those younger than they.[15] The culminating point of this civic generation is the cohort born in 1925–1930, who attended grade school during the Great Depression, spent World War II in high school (or on the battle field), first voted in 1948 or 1952, set up housekeeping in the 1950s, and watched their first television when they were in the late twenties. Since national surveying began, this cohort has been exceptionally civic: voting more, joining more, reading newspapers more, trusting more. As the distinguished

[15]Too few respondents born in the late nineteenth century appear in surveys conducted in the 1970s and 1980s for us to discern differences among successive birth cohorts with great reliability. However, those scant data (not broken out in Figure 1) suggest that the turn of the century might have been an era of rising civic engagement. Similarly, too few respondents born after 1970 have yet appeared in national surveys for us to be confident about their distinctive generational profile, although the slender results so far seem to suggest that the 40-year generational plunge in civic engagement might be bottoming out. However, even if this turns out to be true, it will be several decades before that development could arrest the aggregate drop in civic engagement, for reasons subsequently explained in the text.

sociologist Charles Tilly (born in 1928) said in commenting on an early version of this essay, "we are the last suckers."

To help in interpreting the historical contexts within which these successive generations of Americans matured, Figure 1 also indicates the decade within which each cohort came of age. Thus, we can see that each generation who reached adulthood since the 1940s has been less engaged in community affairs than its immediate predecessor.

Further confirmation of this *generational* interpretation comes from a comparison of the two parallel lines that chart responses to an identical question about social trust, posed first in the National Election Studies (mainly between 1964 and 1976) and then in the General Social Survey between 1972 and 1994.[16] If the greater trust expressed by Americans born earlier in the century represented a *life cycle* effect, then the graph from the GSS surveys (conducted when these cohorts were, on average, ten years older) should have been some distance *above* the NES line. In fact, the GSS line lies about 5–10% *below* the NES line. That downward shift almost surely represents a *period* effect that depressed social trust among all cohorts during the 1980s.[17] That downward period effect, however, is substantially more modest than the large generational differences already noted.

In short, the most parsimonious interpretation of the age-related differences in civic engagement is that they represent a powerful reduction in civic engagement among Americans who came of age in the decades after World War II, as well as some modest additional disengagement that affected all cohorts during the 1980s. These patterns hint that being raised after World War II was a quite different experience from being raised before that watershed. It is as though the postwar generations were exposed

[16]Members of the 1910–1940 generation also seem more civic than their elders, at least to judge by the outlooks of the relatively few men and women born in the late nineteenth century who appeared in our samples.

[17]The questions on social trust appeared biennially in the NES from 1964 to 1976 and then reappeared in 1992. I have included the 1992 NES interviews in the analysis in order to obtain estimates for cohorts too young to have appeared in the earlier surveys.

to some mysterious X-ray that permanently and increasingly rendered them less likely to connect with the community. Whatever that force might have been, *it*—rather than anything that happened during the 1970s and 1980s—accounts for most of the civic disengagement that lies at the core of our mystery. . . .

The Puzzle Reformulated

To say that civic disengagement in contemporary America is in large measure generational merely reformulates our central puzzle. We now know that much of the cause of our lonely bowling probably dates to the 1940s and 1950s, rather than to the 1960s and 1970s. What could have been the mysterious anti-civic "X-ray" that affected Americans who came of age after World War II and whose effects progressively deepened at least into the 1970s?[18] . . .

I have discovered only one prominent suspect against whom circumstantial evidence can be mounted. . . . The culprit is television.

First, the timing fits. The long civic generation was the last cohort of Americans to grow up without television, for television flashed into American society like lightning in the 1950s. In 1950 barely 10% of American homes had television sets, but by 1959 90% did, probably the fastest diffusion of a technological innovation ever recorded. The reverberations from this lightning bolt continued for decades, as viewing hours per capita grew by 17–20% during the 1960s and by an additional 7–8% during the 1970s. In the early years, TV watching was concentrated among the less educated sectors of the population, but during the 1970s the viewing time of the more educated sectors of the population began to converge upward. Television viewing increases with age, particularly upon retirement, but each generation since the introduction of television has begun its life cycle at a higher

---

[18]Additional analysis of indicators of civic engagement in the GSS, not reported in detail here, confirms this downward shift during the 1980s.

starting point. By 1995, viewing per TV household was more than 50% higher than it had been in the 1950s.[19]

Most studies estimate that the average American now watches roughly four hours per day.[20] Robinson (1990b), using the more conservative time-budget technique for determining how people allocate their time, offers an estimate closer to three hours per day, but concludes that as a primary activity, television absorbs 40% of the average American's free time, an increase of about one-third since 1965. Moreover, multiple sets have proliferated: by the late 1980s, three quarters of all U.S. homes had more than one set (Comstock 1989), and these numbers too are rising steadily, allowing ever more private viewing. In short, as Robinson and Godbey 1995 conclude, "television is the 800-pound gorilla of leisure time." This massive change in the way Americans spend our days and nights occurred precisely during the years of generational civic disengagement.

Evidence of a link between the arrival of television and the erosion of social connections is, however, not merely circumstantial. The links between civic engagement and television viewing can instructively be compared with the links between civic engagement and newspaper reading. The basic contrast is

[19]I record here one theory attributed variously to Robert Salisbury (1985), Gerald Gamm, and Simon and Garfunkel. Devotees of our national pastime will recall that Joe Dimaggio signed with the Yankees in 1936, just as the last of the long civic generation was beginning to follow the game, and he turned center field over to Mickey Mantle in 1951, just as the last of "the suckers" reached legal maturity. Almost simultaneously, the Braves, the Athletics, the Browns, the Senators, the Dodgers, and the Giants deserted cities that had been their homes since the late nineteenth century. By the time Mantle in turn left the Yankees in 1968, much of the damage to civic loyalty had been done. This interpretation explains why Mrs. Robinson's plaintive query that year about Joltin' Joe's whereabouts evoked such widespread emotion. A deconstructionist analysis of social capital's decline would highlight the final haunting lamentation, "our nation turns its *lonely* eyes to you" [emphasis added].

[20]For introductions to the massive literature on the sociology of television, see Bower (1985), Comstock et al. (1978), Comstock (1989), and Grabner (1993). The figures on viewing hours in the text are from Bower (1985, 33) and *Public Perspective* (1995, 47). Cohort differences are reported in Bower 1985, 46.

straightforward: newspaper reading is associated with high social capital, TV viewing with low social capital.

Controlling for education, income, age, race, place of residence, work status, and gender, TV viewing is strongly and negatively related to social trust and group membership, whereas the same correlations with newspaper reading are positive. . . . How might television destroy social capital?

- *Time displacement.* Even though there are only 24 hours in everyone's day, most forms of social and media participation are positively correlated. People who listen to lots of classical music are more likely, not less likely, than others to attend Cubs games. Television is the principal exception to this generalization—the only leisure activity that seems to inhibit participation outside the home. TV watching comes at the expense of nearly every social activity outside the home, especially social gatherings and informal conversations (Comstock et al. 1978; Comstock 1989; Bower 1985; and Robinson and Godbey 1995). TV viewers are homebodies. . . .
- One important quasi-experimental study of the introduction of television in three Canadian towns (Williams 1986) found the same pattern at the aggregate level across time: a major effect of television's arrival was the reduction in participation in social, recreational, and community activities among people of all ages. In short, television is privatizing our leisure time.
- *Effects on the outlooks of viewers.* An impressive body of literature, gathered under the rubric of the "mean world effect," suggests that heavy watchers of TV are unusually skeptical about the benevolence of other people—overestimating crime rates, for example. This body of literature has generated much debate about the underlying causal patterns, with skeptics suggesting that misanthropy may foster couch-potato behavior rather than the reverse. While awaiting better experimental evidence, however, a reasonable interim judgment is that heavy television watching may well increase pessimism about human nature (Gerbner et al 1980; Dobb and MacDonald 1979; Hirsh 1980; and Comstock 1989, 265–69). . . .
- *Effects on children.* TV occupies an extraordinary part of children's lives—consuming about 40 hours per week on average. Viewing is especially high among pre-adolescents, but it remains high among younger adolescents: time-budget studies (Carnegie Council on

Adolescent Development 1993, 5, citing Timmer et al. 1985) suggest that among youngsters aged 9–14 television consumes as much time as *all other discretionary activities combined,* including playing, hobbies, clubs, outdoor activities, informal visiting, and just hanging out. The effects of television on childhood socialization have, of course, been hotly debated for more than three decades. The most reasonable conclusion from a welter of sometimes conflicting results appears to be that heavy television watching probably increases aggressiveness (although perhaps not actual violence), that it probably reduces school achievement, and that it is statistically associated with "psychosocial malfunctioning," although how much of this effect is self-selection and how much causal remains much debated (Condry 1993). The evidence is, as I have said, not yet enough to convict, but the defense has a lot of explaining to do.

Conclusion

Ithiel de Sola Pool's posthumous book, *Technologies Without Borders* (1990), is a prescient work, astonishingly relevant to our current national debates about the complicated links among technology, public policy, and culture. Pool defended what he called "soft technological determinism." Revolutions in communications technologies have profoundly affected social life and culture, as the printing press helped bring on the Reformation. Pool concluded that the electronic revolution in communications technology, whose outlines he traced well before most of us were even aware of the impending changes, was the first major technological advance in centuries that would have a profoundly decentralizing and fragmenting effect on society and culture.

Pool hoped that the result might be "community without contiguity." As a classic liberal, he welcomed the benefits of technological change for individual freedom, and, in part, I share that enthusiasm. Those of us who bemoan the decline of community in contemporary America need to be sensitive to the liberating gains achieved during the same decades. We need to avoid an uncritical nostalgia for the Fifties. On the other hand, some of the same freedom-friendly technologies whose rise Pool predicted may indeed be undermining our connections with one another and with our communities. I suspect that Pool would have been open to that argument, too, for one of Pool's most talented protégés, Samuel Popkin (1991, 226–31) has argued that the rise of television and the correlative decline of social interaction have impaired American political discourse. The last line in Pool's last book (1990, 262) is this: "We may suspect that [the technological trends that we can anticipate] will promote individualism and will make it harder, not easier, to govern and organize a coherent society."

Pool's technological determinism was "soft" precisely because he recognized that social values can condition the effects of technology. In the end this perspective invites us not merely to consider how technology is privatizing our lives—if, as it seems to me, it is—but to ask whether we entirely like the result, and if not, what we might do about it. But that is a topic for another day.

References

Bower, Robert T. 1985. *The Changing Television Audience in America*. New York: Columbia University Press.

Brehm, John, and Wendy Rahn. 1995. "An Audit of the Deficit in Social Capital." Durham, NC: Duke University. Unpublished manuscript.

Butler, David, and Donald Stokes. 1974. *Political Change in Britain: The Evolution of Electoral Choice*, 2nd ed. New York: St. Martin's.

Caplow, Theodore, Howard M. Bahr, John Modell, and Bruce A. Chadwick. 1991. *Recent Social Trends in the United States: 1960–1990*. Montreal: McGill-Queen's University Press.

Carnegie Council on Adolescent Development. 1993. *A Matter of Time: Risk and Opportunity in the Nonschool Hours: Executive Summary*. New York: Carnegie Corporation of New York.

Coleman, James. 1990. *Foundations of Social Theory*. Cambridge, MA: Harvard University Press.

Comstock, George. 1989. *The Evolution of American Television*. Newbury Park, CA: Sage.

Comstock, George, Steven Chaffee, Natan Katzman, Maxwell McCombs, and Donald Roberts. 1978. *Television and Human Behavior*. New York: Columbia University Press.

Condry, John. 1993. "Thief of Time, Unfaithful Servant: Television and the American Child," *Daedalus* 122 (Winter): 259–78.

Converse, Philip E. 1976. *The Dynamics of Party Support: Cohort-Analyzing Party Identification*. Beverly Hills, CA: Sage.

Cutler, Blaine. 1990. "Where Does the Free Time Go?" *American Demographics* (November): 36–39.

Davis, James Allan, and Tom W. Smith. *General Social Surveys, 1972–1994.* [machine readable data file]. Principal Investigator, James A. Davis; Director and Co-Principal Investigator, Tom W. Smith. NORC ed. Chicago: National Opinion Research Center, producer, 1994; Storrs, CT: The Roper Center for Public Opinion Research, University of Connecticut, distributor.

Dobb, Anthony N., and Glenn F. Macdonald. 1979. "Television Viewing and Fear of Victimization: Is the Relationship Causal?" *Journal of Personality and Social Psychology* 37:170–79.

Edwards, Patricia Klobus, John N. Edwards, and Ann DeWitt Watts, "Women, Work, and Social Participation." *Journal of Voluntary Action Research* 13 (January–March, 1984), 7–22.

Elazar, Daniel J. 1966. *American Federalism: A View from the States.* New York: Crowell.

Fukuyama, Francis. 1995. *Trust: The Social Virtues and the Creation of Prosperity.* New York: The Free Press.

Gerbner, George, Larry Gross, Michael Morgan, and Nancy Signorielli. 1980. "The 'Mainstreaming' of America: Violence Profile No. 11," *Journal of Communication* 30 (Summer): 10–29.

Ginzberg, Eli. *The Unemployed.* 1943. New York: Harper and Brothers.

Glenn, Norval D. 1987. "Social Trends in the United States: Evidence from Sample Surveys." *Public Opinion Quarterly* 51: S109–S126.

Grabner, Doris A. 1993. *Mass Media and American Politics.* Washington, D.C.: CQ Press.

Hirsch, Paul M. "The 'Scary World' of the Nonviewer and Other Anomalies: A Reanalysis of Gerbner et al.'s Findings on Cultivation Analysis, Part I," *Communication Research* 7 (October): 403–56.

Hughes, Michael. 1980. "The Fruits of Cultivation Analysis: A Re-examination of the Effects of Television Watching on Fear of Victimization, Alienation, and the Approval of Violence." *Public Opinion Quarterly* 44: 287–303.

Jahoda, Marie, Paul Lazarsfeld, and Hans Zeisel. 1933. *Marienthal.* Chicago: Aldine-Atherton.

Mannheim, Karl. 1952. "The Problem of Generations." In *Essays on the Sociology of Knowledge,* ed. Paul Kécskemeti. New York: Oxford University Press: 276–322.

Meyrowitz, Joshua. 1985. *No sense of Place: The Impact of Electronic Media on Social Behavior.* New York: Oxford University Press.

Miller, Warren E. 1992. "The Puzzle Transformed: Explaining Declining Turnout." *Political Behaviour* 14: 1–43.

Miller, Warren F., and J. Merrill Shanks. 1995. *The American Voter Reconsidered*. Tempe, AZ: Arizona State University. Unpublished manuscript.

Pool, Ithiel de Sola. 1973. "Public Opinion." In *Handbook of Communication*, ed. Ithiel de Sola Pool et al. Chicago: Rand McNally: 779–835.

Pool, Ithiel de Sola. 1990. *Technologies Without Boundaries: On Telecommunications in a Global Age*. Cambridge, MA: Harvard University Press.

Popkin, Samuel L. 1991. *The Reasoning Voter*. Chicago: University of Chicago Press.

Postman, Neil. 1985. *Amusing Ourselves to Death: Public Discourse in the Age of Show Business*. New York: Viking-Penguin Books.

Public Perspective. 1995. "People, Opinion, and Polls: American Popular Culture." 6 (August/September): 37–48.

Putnam, Robert D. 1993. *Making Democracy Work: Civic Traditions in Modern Italy*. Priceton, NJ: Princeton University Press.

Putnam, Robert D. 1995. "Bowling Alone, Revisited," *The Responsive Community* (Spring): 18–33.

Putnam, Robert D. 1996. "Bowling Alone: Democracy in America at the End of the Twentieth Century," forthcoming in a collective volume edited by Axel Hadenius. New York: Cambridge University Press.

Robinson, John. 1981. "Television and Leisure Time: A New Scenario," *Journal of Communication* 31 (Winter): 120–30.

Robinson, John. 1990a. "The Time Squeeze," *American Demographics* (February).

Robinson, John. 1990b. " I Love My TV." *American Demographics* (September): 24–27.

Robinson, John, and Geoffrey Godbey. 1995. *Time for Life*. College Park, MD: University of Maryland. Unpublished manuscript.

Rosenstone, Steven J., and John Mark Hansen. 1993. *Mobilization, Participation, and Democracy in America*. New York: Macmillan.

Salisbury, Robert H. 1985. "Blame Dismal World Conditions on . . . Baseball." *Miami Herald* (May 18): 27A.

Schor, Juliet. 1991. *The Overworked American*. New York: Basic Books.

Sharkansky, Ira. 1969. "The Utility of Elazar's Political Culture." *Polity* 2: 66–83.

The Economist. 1995. "The Solitary Bowler." 334 (18 February): 21–22.

Timmer, S. G., J. Eccles, and I. O'Brien. 1985. "How Children Use Time." In *Time, Goods, and Well-Being*, ed. F. T. Juster and F. B. Stafford. Ann Arbor, MI: University of Michigan, Institute for Social Research.

U.S. Bureau of the Census. 1995 (and earlier years). *Current Population Reports*. Washington, D.C.

Verba, Sidney, Kay Lehman Schlozman, and Henry E. Brady. 1995. *Voice and Equality: Civic Volunteerism in American Politics*. Cambridge, MA: Harvard University Press.

Wilcock, Richard, and Walter H. Franke. 1963. *Unwanted Workers*. New York: Free Press of Glencoe.

Williams, Tannis Macbeth, ed. 1986. *The Impact of Television: A Natural Experiment in Three Communities*. New York: Academic Press.

About the Author

Robert D. Putnam is Clarence Dillon Professor of International Affairs and Director, Center for International Affairs, Harvard University. His 1993 book *Making Democracy Work: Civic Traditions in Modern Italy* (Princeton University Press) won the 1994 Gregory Luebbert Award from the Comparative Politics Organized Section of the APSA.

APPENDIX B

MINORITY REPRESENTATION UNDER CUMULATIVE AND LIMITED VOTING*

DAVID BROCKINGTON
University of Washington

TODD DONOVAN
Western Washington University

SHAUN BOWLER
University of California, Riverside

ROBERT BRISCHETTO
University of Texas, San Antonio

We examine minority representation resulting from modified at-large elections (cumulative and limited voting) used in U.S. localities in the 1990s. Hypotheses about the relative proportionality of descriptive representation under various local election systems are presented and tested. We find that CV/LV elections produced descriptive representation of African-Americans at levels similar to those in larger single-member district places, and at levels that exceed those from some small, southern SMD places. Results for Latino representation are more qualified. Our results offer encouragement for those interested in facilitating minority representation without using the acrimonious process of drawing districts on the basis of races.

The Journal of Politics, Vol. 60, No. 4, November 1998, pp. 1108–25 © 1998 by the University of Texas Press, P.O. Box 7819, Austin, TX 78713–7819. Reprinted with permission of Blackwell Publishing.

Recent decisions of the United States Supreme Court have directed increased attention at alternatives to districting for the purpose of minority representation (see Pildes and Donoghue 1995). In this paper we assess how modified at-large plans (limited and cumulative voting) might facilitate minority representation. We also examine how representation under these plans compares to that obtained with district and at-large elections.

In previous decades, court interpretations of the Voting Rights Act (VRA) broadened the ability of the U.S. Department of Justice and minority plaintiffs to challenge local election plans that might dilute minority vote strength (i.e., *Thornburg v. Gingles* 1986; *Gomez v. Watsonville* 1988). The plans most often subject to challenge include councils elected under multimember, at-large systems. The standard remedy in these situations has been changing to single-member district (SMD) plans, with districts drawn to facilitate minority representation. Indeed, a substantial body of evidence demonstrates that racial and ethnic minorities are more likely to win seats proportionate to their share of the population in districted jurisdictions (Engstrom and McDonald 1981; Polinard, Wrinkle, and Longoria 1991; Welch 1990).

Limits to Districting as a Remedy

Districting on the basis of race, however, has come under increased scrutiny by the courts. The *Shaw v. Reno* decision (1993) criticized "bizarre"-shaped districts. *Miller v. Johnson* (1995) found a majority-minority congressional district unconstitutional and argued that districts should not be drawn based "on race in substantial disregard of customary and traditional districting practices." *Shaw v. Hunt* (1996) and *Bush v. Vera* (1996) found separate districting plans in violation of the Fourteenth Amendment's equal protection clause. When race is found to be the "predominant factor" in districting, the contemporary Court must apply the strict scrutiny test for the equal protection clause. This makes it extremely difficult for state and local governments to establish a compelling interest in adopting such districts.

Majority-minority districts have also come under criticism since they may "waste" votes (Lijphart 1994; Still 1984). Others suggest that districting can limit minority influence over policy (Guinier 1991, 1994; Sass and Mehay n.d.) and prevent the formation of coalitions across racial lines (Swain 1993). There are practical problems as well. Edward Still (1991) notes that districts drawn with a 65% African-American population are perhaps the bare minimum required to facilitate African-American representation in some instances, although Brace et al. (1988) note that this minimum varies greatly by place.

Cumulative and Limited Voting in the United States

In response to the perceived limits of districting, cumulative voting (CV) and limited voting (LV) have been proposed as a means of increasing minority representation. A number of small- and medium-sized U.S. jurisdictions have adopted these plans (Amy 1993; Cole and Taebel 1992; Cole, Taebel, and Engstrom 1990; Still 1984, 1991).[1] Both systems operate to elect multimember councils at-large and facilitate proportionality by changing how voters cast ballots.

Several jurisdictions in North Carolina, Alabama, and Texas adopted modified at-large systems (and to a lesser extent, places in New Mexico, South Dakota, and Illinois). Over 75 city councils, county councils, and school boards had adopted CV or LV at the time of this writing.[2] These elections create relatively low thresholds of exclusion—the proportion of votes that a group

---

[1]There is only one jurisdiction in the United States with a population over 100,000 using a CV or LV system: Peoria, Illinois.

[2]Details about each jurisdiction's system were identified with phone calls to local officials in each place. Communications with local officials and individuals involved with VRA litigation led to the identification of these communities. Several additional places are in the process of settling lawsuits that will result in the adoption of limited or cumulative voting.

needs to elect one candidate assuming all the group's voters support the candidate. In a CV election for a five-member council, for example, a minority candidate with 17% support could not be denied a seat.

Under LV, voters are restricted to fewer votes than seats up for election. Candidates are elected by plurality, and candidates with the most votes win until seats are filled. In party systems, outcomes under LV are expected to be more proportionate the more limited the vote is relative to the number of seats at stake (for a description see Lakeman 1970, 80–88; Still 1984, 253–55). Cumulative voting modifies at-large plans by allowing voters to cast as many votes as seats being elected, with the additional option of clustering votes among any combination of candidates. The voter may typically distribute votes in any way she feels, including distributing them across fewer candidates than available seats. Candidates are elected by plurality, and candidates with the most votes win until seats are filled. . . .

Strategic Burdens under Limited and Cumulative Voting

There are reasons to expect some deviations from proportionate descriptive representation in CV and LV places. CV and LV are often labeled as "semiproportionate" in classifications of electoral systems (Amy 1993; Lakeman 1970). Much of the potential for these modified at-large plans to produce deviations from proportionality lies in the demands for strategic coordination (Cox 1997) that each system places at the mass and elite level. Under each system, a party or slating group must effectively maximize seats by controlling the candidate selection process such that they place an optimal number of candidates on the ballot. To optimize representation, the groups must also spread their supporters' votes accurately across those candidates they nominate (Still 1984, 254–55). . . . If a group overnominates and lists too many candidates, it risks spreading the votes of supporters too thin, causing underrepresentation. If a group undernominates, it errs by possibly wasting votes that might have yielded another seat.

. . . A minority group often need only nominate one candidate to insure some representation (or simply nominate as many candidates as votes allowed). . . . Control of nominations under CV might be required for proportionate descriptive representation of minority groups, but CV further modifies at-large plans in a manner that can produce an additional strategic burden for minority groups. With CV, groups must coordinate their supporters' voting behavior to discourage voters from spreading their multiple votes in a manner that disperses electoral strength. In other words, voters must be informed about the optimal strategy of clustering votes among candidates. Plainly, CV can require strategic coordination at both the mass (vote distribution) and elite (nomination) levels, while LV might require less coordination if the vote is limited to one. As a result, Still (1984, 256) suggests that CV is likely to require more strategic voting than LV to achieve proportional results (on the possibility of strategic mistakes by minority voters in CV; see also Engstrom 1993).

Since CV allows voters more options when delivering their votes, the existence of such opportunities increases the probability that some minority voters will spread votes across multiple candidates, even if only one minority candidate is running. This, in turn, increases the chance that minority votes might go to nonminority candidates, potentially limiting the translation of minority vote strength into seats.[3] Furthermore, in CV or LV places where a group's population share is near the threshold of exclusion and voting is racially polarized, minority candidates can only be elected if their supporters turn out at a rate matching majority-group voters. All of this suggests that descriptive representation of minorities under CV might be somewhat less proportionate to population than that obtained under LV.

[3]Surveys from a city using CV illustrated that 36% of Latino voters used the option to cast at least one of their votes for a non-Latino candidate (Cole, Taebel, and Engstrom 1990; Cole and Taebel 1992).

There are reasons to expect that each plan could produce less proportionate descriptive representation than SMD systems. With SMD plans, if cartographers have the ability to tailor boundaries to create heavily minority districts, and they create a number of minority districts in proportion to overall minority vote share in a jurisdiction, then proportionate descriptive representation can be expected. Compared to CV/LV, once homogeneous majority-minority districts are created, limited strategic behavior is required of elites (e.g., mobilization of minority voters in numbers approaching majority-group turnout and controlling nominations), and little strategic electoral behavior is required of voters (e.g., vote dispersion) to produce proportionate descriptive representation.[4] In other words, districting can institutionalize some of the strategic actions needed to facilitate minority representation, and could possibly produce greater minority representation than CV/LV systems.

Hypotheses: Outcomes under Modified At-Large Voting

The discussion above suggests several testable propositions about how the seats–population relationship in modified at-large (alternative) elections compares to those obtained under districting and to unmodified at-large (AL) plans, and how LV and CV alternatives compare to each other.

First, we expect that modified at-large systems (CV and LV) should produce more-proportionate representation of minorities than that resulting from the traditional at-large method. Assuming that a group votes roughly as a block, any group winning a plurality is likely to sweep all seats in an unmodified at-large election

---

[4]Optimal districting arrangements are a possibility where minority groups are highly segregated spatially. Since African-American housing is historically more segregated from whites than Latino housing (Massey and Denton 1987), districting might produce more-proportionate representation of African-Americans than of Latinos (Taebel 1978; see also Vedlitz and Johnson 1982).

(Lakeman 1970). Although nearly every electoral system has bias in favor of the group gaining the largest vote share in an election, the bias is greatest under American-style at-large, plurality systems (Johnson 1979). Conversely, both LV and CV have lower minimum thresholds than at-large elections. . . .

Second, given strategic demands and the "semiproportionate" nature of CV/LV, we expect that modified at-large elections might produce less-proportionate descriptive representation of minorities than SMD elections.[5] Modified at-large plans can facilitate minority representation by lowering the threshold of votes required for a minority candidate to win office, but groups must be fairly well organized politically to take advantage of these systems. SMD plans might facilitate minority representation with less coordination requirements for elites and voters.

Third, limited voting might be expected to produce more-proportionate outcomes than cumulative voting. This hypothesis is based on the assumption that the latter system can require an additional element of strategic behavior (coordination of vote dispersion) from voters and elites.

Data and Framework for Analysis

Cases for our tests are drawn from U.S. cities, counties, and school districts that adopted CV or LV in response to actual or anticipated VRA lawsuits. Since we are interested in estimating how electoral systems are related to representation of minority groups relative to their share of the local population, we limited our analysis to jurisdictions for which 1990 census population data are available. Initial information on local election systems

---

[5]This logic does not suggest that any (national) electoral system using winner-take-all, single-member districts would ever produce more-proportionate outcomes than a multimember LV or CV system. It is important to note that the difference in proportionality we expect is not so much a function of single-member districts per se, but of the appointment of racial and ethnic groups into particular districts.

and election results were obtained in the spring of 1995 via telephone interviews with city clerks and county election officials, with additional data acquired in subsequent interviews in 1996 and 1997. Nearly all the places we identified are located in three states: Texas, Alabama, and North Carolina. South Dakota, New Mexico, and Illinois each also have a single jurisdiction that used CV. We limit our analysis to places from these six states where the predominant minority made up less than 50% of the voting population.

We treat individual elections as cases. This allows us greater comparability in our analysis, largely because this diffuses the problem created by those jurisdictions that stagger elections. We include the two most recent elections from each jurisdiction in the analysis, or the most recent if the jurisdiction had only one CV or LV contest as of spring 1997. This allows us to capture variation in elections across places and within places, since most of these communities alternate the number of seats contested in consecutive elections. Data from nearly all these places involve elections contested between 1994 and 1997, although the second most recent elections in three places were held between 1990 and 1992.

The dependent variable is the percentage of CV or LV seats won by minority candidates in each election. Our models thus isolate the seats–population unique relationship to modified at-large elections, and eliminate from the analysis those seats elected in these communities by other methods.[6] Communities included in the seats–population analysis were limited to places with a population of more than 1,000, the minimum for racial information to be included in census data. Most communities are rather small, with a median population of 3,167 and a mean of 10,311. The resulting sample used to assess the seats–population relationship includes a total of 62 jurisdictions offering data for 96 elections.

---

[6]For example, if a place was electing five seats via CV (or LV) in an election, the dependent variable would be calculated as # CV seats won by minority candidates/5. Likewise, if a place elected three seats via districts, and two via CV, the dependent variable would be # CV seats won by minority candidates/2.

TABLE 1   RACIAL/ETHNIC DISTRIBUTION OF CASES

Predominant Minority Group	Total Number of Elections	Elections with Minority Candidates	Elections with Minority Victory
Latino	66	47 (71%)[a]	33 (50%)[a] (70%)[b]
African-American	28	26 (93%)[a]	25 (89%)[a] (96%)[b]
Native-American	02	01 (50%)[a]	00 (0%)[ab]

[a]Percentage of all elections.

[b]Percentage of elections where minority candidates sought office.

NOTE: Cases are individual elections. Data are from the two most recent elections, or the most recent elections if the jurisdiction had only one CV/LV contest as of 1997.

Table 1 demonstrates that minorities have had success contesting these elections, despite low levels of representation prior to the change in election systems. A Latino candidate was elected in 70% of the contests where a Latino candidate sought office under CV. Further, in 96% of CV/LV elections where an African-American sought office, at least one African-American was elected. Table 1 also illustrates something that will be discussed below: in elections where the predominant minority was Latino, Latino candidates were on the ballot in only 71% of elections.

Hypotheses about how elections translate minority voting age population share into minority seats on local councils can be tested by regressing seats against population (Engstrom and McDonald 1981). Bivariate regression produces slope estimates that can be used to assess differences in seats–population relationships across electoral systems, and can be compared to those produced by other studies using the same method. For example, when percentage data are used, a slope of 1.0 with an intercept of 0 indicates that minority seat shares on local councils occur in exact proportion to the percent of the local voting age population that is minority. . . .

TABLE 2   MINORITY SEATS–POPULATION RELATIONSHIP
UNDER CUMULATIVE AND LIMITED VOTING

Variables	Model 2.1 (All)	Model 2.2 (Black)	Model 2.3 (Latino)	Model 2.4 (LV)
Minority %VAP	.15	.95°°°	.03	.01
	(.18)	(.13)	(.21)	(.18)
LV Dummy	—	—	—	−.19
				(.15)
LV°Min%VAP	—	—	—	1.12°
				(.48)
Intercept	.15°°	.04	.16	.17°°
	(.06)	(.08)	(.07)	(.06)
R^2	.01	.26	.00	.12[a]
Number of Cases	96	28	66	96

[a]R^2 for model 2.4 is adjusted; all others unadjusted.

°°$p < .05$; °°°$p < .01$ (two-tailed t-tests)

NOTE: Dependent variable = number CV/LV council seats won by minorities divided by number of CV/LV seats in election. VAP is voting age population. Cell entries are unstandardized regression coefficients, or the slope of the relationship between the dependent and independent variables.

As shown in Table 2, models are first estimated for all CV and LV jurisdictions, including cases where the predominant minority group is either African-American, Latino, or Native American[7] (model 2.1). We then estimate separate models for African-American and Latino places to assess if modified at-large voting is associated with a different seats–population relationship for these groups (models 2.2 and 2.3, respectively). We also estimate a multivariate model with all cases using an interaction term and dummy variable to test if minority representation is more common under LV than CV (model 2.4). To evaluate our other hypotheses, the slopes resulting from these models are compared

[7]In a single CV jurisdiction (Sisseton, SD school district) the predominant minority group is Native American.

to those produced from other studies. This can provide some idea of how minority representation under modified at-large elections compares to other electoral systems used in U.S. localities.

Information about the slope of these relationships can be more important than a simple demonstration that more minorities serve on these local councils after changing to modified at-large voting. Each of these jurisdictions adopted new electoral systems because they had sizable minority populations with very limited (or in many places no) minority representation. Only two of these places have minority populations under 10% (the lowest being 7%).[8] In many (if not most) of the jurisdictions included in our analysis, minority representation increased under modified at-large voting. Our models illustrate the systematic nature of this process in a manner that facilitates comparison with studies of other electoral systems.

Results

Results from model 2.1 indicate that when all modified at-large jurisdictions are examined simultaneously, there is a poor fit between minority population and percent of seats controlled by the minority groups. Variation in seats–population relationships across modified at-large places is evident when we examine African-American and Latino jurisdictions separately. The fit of

[8]For example, Thomas and Stewart (1988, 171) note that 44% of Alabama Black Belt counties examined in a 1982 federal study (U.S. Civil Rights Commission 1983, cited in Thomas and Stewart 1988) had no black representation. Many of these counties having no black representation had majority-black populations. A number of our towns are drawn from these counties. Each of the North Carolina places using LV were also in VRA-targeted areas since 1964. Keech and Sistrom (1994) report that 90% of North Carolina counties and cities were unmodified at-large as of 1989. Blacks were heavily underrepresented in these places. In places where blacks were a minority, representational equity scores did not exceed .20. Nearly all of our North Carolina cases come from these communities.

the model is greatly improved ($R^2 = .26$) when African-American jurisdictions are examined in isolation (R^2 increases to .45 when the analysis is restricted to cases with black candidates). Model 2.2 illustrates that for these places, the relationship between seats and minority voting age population is represented by a slope of .95 and an intercept not significantly different than zero. Thus, in those elections where the primary minority is African-American, as the minority percentage of the population increases, a nearly equivalent gain in descriptive representation is achieved. Furthermore, since the intercept is near zero, population share is translated into representation at low levels of minority population.

Model 2.3 reports the slope of the seats–population relationship for places where the predominant minority is Latino. Given the insignificant slope and the very low R^2, there does not appear to be a substantive linear relationship between minority population share and minority seat share on councils and school boards. This does not mean that Latino candidates were not elected in places that adopted modified at-large voting. As with majority-African-American jurisdictions, Latino candidates were elected in greater numbers after switching to modified at-large. As reported in Table 1, where Latino candidates sought office, they were successful in over half (33 out of 47) of these cases—marking a dramatic improvement over the previous levels of Latino representation in these communities (Brischetto 1995; Brischetto and Engstrom 1998). Nevertheless, elections in many places with substantial Latino populations produced no Latino representation due to both a lack of candidates [and] defeat at the polls. Even when the analysis is restricted to cases where Latino candidates sought office (not reported here), there is still no significant effect. In the discussion section we address how seats–population models can underestimate the potential for Latino representation.

We hypothesized that these new modified at-large systems would produce more-proportionate descriptive representation of minorities than standard at-large plans, and less-proportionate

FIGURE 1   CV/LV SEATS–POPULATION RELATIONSHIP COMPARED
            TO OTHER SYSTEMS, U.S. SOUTH

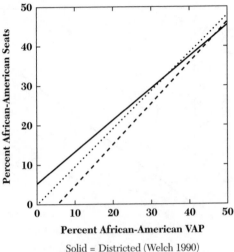

Solid = Districted (Welch 1990)
Dashed = At-Large (Welch 1990)
Dotted = Modified At-Large (CV/LV)

representation than SMD plans. Our results are put into perspective by comparing the results from our models to those from other studies examining local election systems in the United States. If we compare our slope and intercept for African-American representation under modified at-large systems to those from previous studies of standard at-large systems, we find some support for these hypotheses.

As Figure 1 illustrates, the seats–population relationship for African-Americans under recently modified at-large voting is similar to that found by Welch (1990) for African-Americans in larger (over 50,000 residents) southern cities using SMD where blacks are a minority of the population. Figure 1 compares our results from model 2.2 to Welch's findings. Across much of the range in minority population, it appears modified (CV/LV)

FIGURE 2   CV/LV SEATS–POPULATION RELATIONSHIP COMPARED
TO OTHER SYSTEMS, SMALL SOUTHERN PLACES

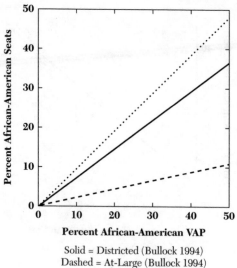

Solid = Districted (Bullock 1994)
Dashed = At-Large (Bullock 1994)
Dotted = Modified At-Large (CV/LV)

plans (represented by the dotted line) produce similar levels of representation as districting (the solid line), and slightly greater descriptive representation than standard at-large plans (the dashed line).

Since nearly all of our cases come from elections in relatively small places that recently switched election systems, Welch's data might not be best suited for comparing seats–population relationships across systems. When we compare our estimates to those from a study of other southern places that had recently switched away from AL plans—a study that includes many smaller, rural places more similar to communities in this study—levels of African-American representation under modified at-large plans appear more striking. Bullock (1994) examined elections to county commissions in Georgia in 1991. Of the counties studied, 52 used SMD plans, an increase from 17 in

1981.[9] Figure 2 plots Bullock's bivariate seats–registration relationship in SMD places (the solid line) and the relationship we estimated in model 2.2 for African-American jurisdictions using CV/LV plans (the dotted line). The plot demonstrates results contrary to one of our hypotheses—modified at-large elections actually produced slightly *more*-proportionate outcomes when compared to these districted places.

The differences between standard at-large elections and CV/LV elections are substantial when we compare our estimates to those from Bullock's study of Georgia counties, and are consistent with the hypothesis that CV/LV plans will produce more-proportionate representation of minorities than traditional AL systems. The dashed line represents the bivariate seats–registration relationship for the 41 Georgia counties still using unmodified AL elections in 1991. Compared to these cases, modified at-large systems produced substantially greater descriptive representation for African-Americans.[10]

Our last hypothesis dealt with the difference between outcomes under LV versus CV systems. Since LV plans might involve fewer strategic burdens (e.g., vote dispersion coordination), we expected that LV systems could produce greater minority representation than CV. Model 2.4 included a coefficient reflecting

---

[9]Like the cases in our study then, many of these places had recently moved away from AL plans in response to actual or potential VRA action under Section 2. As with our study, Bullock's cases were limited to places where African-Americans were in the minority ($N=149$ counties). Given the recent election system changes in many of these places, and the small population and rural nature of many, we suggest they are a good basis for making comparisons with our study.

[10]Differences between our estimates from CV/LV and Bullock's estimates from AL and SMD are even more striking when we consider that our models use percent minority voting age population as the key independent variable, while Bullock uses percent minority voter registration. Given the gap between population and voter registration, our estimates could have been expected to be biased against finding proportionate relationships, which would be evident when registration data are used.

the interaction between a dummy representing LV places and minority voting age population. In theory, this coefficient isolates the unique seats–population relationship for LV. The significant coefficient for the interaction term (1.12; $p < .05$) can be seen as reflecting greater proportionate descriptive representation of minorities when comparing LV to CV places. This is consistent with assumptions that lower strategic demands are required for effective use of LV.

It is important to stress that there are relatively few cases of LV elections in the analysis in Table 2 ($N = 17$), and all are in places where the predominant minority is African-American.[11] The interaction in model 2.4 could possibly capture the difference between African-American representation under LV and Latino and African-American representation under CV.

Another way to determine if minorities achieve higher representation under LV is to estimate the seats–population slope for the 28 places with African-American minorities. As shown in Table 3, we first estimate the seats–population slope unique to these places using CV (model 3.1), then compare this to the slope for African-American places using LV (model 3.2). These results are reported in Table 3. Again, we find evidence suggesting a more-proportionate (or overproportionate) relationship between minority population and seats in LV elections ($b = 1.12$, $p = .08$) than in CV elections ($b = .60$, $p < .05$).[12] However, the population–seats coefficient under LV is not significantly larger than the coefficient under CV. The slope and intercept values for the population–seats model in Table 3 do suggest that CV communities elect black candidates at about the same rate as the districted places analyzed by Bullock as black populations approach

---

[11]All of the variation in election plans occurred across African-American places.

[12]A t-test of the difference between these slopes produces no significant difference. The power of the test is constrained by the small sample. When an interaction term (LV° minority%VAP) is included with all 28 cases from Table 3, the coefficient is positive ($b = .52$) but not significant.

TABLE 3   AFRICAN-AMERICAN SEATS-POPULATION RELATIONSHIP
UNDER CUMULATIVE AND LIMITED VOTING

	Model 3.1	*Model 3.2*
Variables	*(CV Only)*	*(LV Only)*
Minority %VAP	.60°°	1.12°
	(.25)	(.61)
Intercept	.10°°	−.02
	(.04)	(.19)
R^2	.38	.19
Number of Cases	11	17

°p < 10; °°p < .05 (two-tailed t-tests)

NOTE: Dependent variable = number CV/LV council seats won by minorities divided by number of CV/LV seats in election. Cell entries are unstandardized regression coefficients.

50%. At lower ranges of black population, the intercept from model 3.1 indicates that CV produces greater representation than Bullock's SMD places.

There are many additional elements of election system variation that cannot be captured by these dummy variables (degree to which vote is limited, proportion of all seats elected CV or LV, years that jurisdiction has been using CV or LV etc.). Given limited degrees of freedom here, we cannot include these terms and thus cannot conclude with certainty that LV as practiced in the United States produces more-proportionate representation of minorities than CV.

Finally, we should note that there are reasons to expect that the number of seats being contested should affect proportionality for any election system (Lijphart 1994). We did include this as an independent valuable in preliminary models, but the effect was not significant. Since our goal is replicating models from other studies that did not include this measure, we do not include the term in models reported here. There is limited variance in number of seats contested among these elections, so it is difficult to evaluate the effect of this variable.

Discussion

Our data provide evidence that modifying local at-large elections with limited or cumulative voting offers the promise of minority representation at levels very similar to those found under SMD. This finding should be encouraging to those interested in facilitating minority representation without relying upon the acrimonious process of drawing districts on the basis of race. Previous research has established that minorities do win seats under those modified plans. Our purpose was to identify how the seats–population relationship under CV/LV compares to those produced under other plans. For African-Americans, representation from CV/LV elections compares favorably to that obtained from SMD, and is more proportionate than representation under unmodified at-large. For Latinos in communities studied here, this might not be the case.

Our results from Latino places raise questions about why CV election outcomes are less than proportionate. In the cases examined here, underproportionality reflected by our estimates is likely related to a function of three main factors: (1) limited recruitment of Latino candidates, (2) a substantial gap between census measures of Latino voting age population (the key independent variable in these models) and actual rates of Latino participation in elections, and (3) the high threshold of exclusion built into CV plans adopted in many places where Latinos are the predominant minority.

Among our cases are a number of Texas CV elections ($N = 33$) having substantial Latino populations but achieving no Latino representation. In 19 of these cases, clerks indicated that no minority candidates filed for office. Likewise, there were only two cases where African-Americans comprised the predominant minority group and no African-American candidate sought office. Since the data reveal that the nomination problem is more substantial for Latino jurisdictions, under-nomination can partially explain the lack of a linear relationship between seats and population share in majority-Latino jurisdictions.

There were also 14 cases where Latino candidates were defeated in places with significant Latino populations. A second major factor affecting our ability to estimate representation of Latinos in modified at-large systems was the use of census measures of voting age population. In most of the Latino places included in this analysis, Latino turnout was far lower than white turnout.[13] Percent minority VAP data is likely to produce a lower estimated slope than would result had registration or turnout data been used, since these latter variables more accurately reflect minority electoral strength. The gap between census measures of voting age population and actual turnout rates is also likely to be smaller for African-American than for Lations. When Latino turnout data were included in a model limited to the 14 Texas communities where such data are available and in which Latino candidates sought office in 1995, the slope for the Latino seats–turnout relationship is 1.22 (R^2 = .30), and the result was statistically significant.[14] This demonstrates that Latino candidates can do well under CV when Latino voters are mobilized.

Compounding the population–turnout gap is a third factor. Most places in Texas tended to have only two or three CV seats up in any single election. All but two of the Latino cases in the analysis came from Texas. This means that the threshold of exclusion is typically either 25% or 33% in Texas. Low minority turnout will be particularly problematic when this threshold is this high.

We should stress that none of these factors explaining lower rates of Latino representation are an automatic result of the use

---

[13]In two of these jurisdictions, minority turnout actually exceeded Anglo turnout and minority candidates were elected. Turnout data are reported in Brischetto and Engstrom 1998.

[14]1995 is the only year that turnout data by ethnic group are available for Texas places using CV. Latino candidates sought office in 15 Texas CV elections that year, and registration data were reported for 14 of these places. We are thus unable to prepare similar estimates using all 96 cases. These data are available in Brischetto and Engstrom 1998.

of modified at-large electoral systems. Rather, the constraints lie in how some CV plans were designed, and how groups utilize the system. If no more than two seats are contested via CV in an election, it will be difficult for any minority to gain seats unless the minority votes as a block, controls a relatively large share of voting age population (near or greater than 33%), *and* mobilizes voters to turn out at rates matching or exceeding the majority group's voters.

If, however, the election plan creates a threshold that does not exceed the minority group's electoral strength, and a minority political group is organized such that it can recruit candidates, perhaps have some control over nominations, and/or mobilize voters to direct all their votes to specific candidate(s), then many of the strategic burdens associated with CV/LV can be overcome. Our results suggest that these burdens are clearly surmountable, and that CV/LV plans do facilitate proportionate descriptive representation of minority groups under easily obtainable conditions while avoiding the use of race-conscious districting. Our results suggest that many of the potential strategic burdens and coordination requirements associated with CV are readily overcome by minority candidates.

References

Amy, Douglas. 1993. *Real Choices, New Voices.* New York: Columbia University Press.

Brace, Kimball, Bernard Grofman, Lisa Handley, and Richard Niemi. 1988. "Minority Voting Equality; The 65 Percent Rule in Theory and Practice." *Law and Policy* 10(1):43–62.

Brischetto, Robert. 1995. "The Rise of Cumulative Voting." *Texas Obserser,* 28 July, 6.

Brischetto, Robert, and Richard Engstrom. 1998. "Cumulative Voting and Latino Representation: Exit Surveys in Fifteen Texas Communities." *Social Science Quarterly.*

Bullock, Charles S. 1994. "Section 2 of the Voting Rights Act, Districting Formats, and the Election of African-Americans." *Journal of Politics* 56:1098–1105.

Cole, Richard, and Delbert Taebel. 1992. "Cumulative Voting in Local Elections: Lessons from the Alamagordo Experience." *Social Science Quarterly* 73:194–201.

Cole, Richard, Delbert Taebel, and Richard Engstrom. 1990. "Cumulative Voting in a Municipal Election: A Note on Voter Reactions and Electoral Consequences." *Western Political Quarterly* 43(4):191–99.

Cox, Gary. 1997. *Making Votes Count*. Cambridge: Cambridge University Press.

Engstrom, Richard. 1993. "The Single-Transferable Vote: An Alternative Remedy for Minority Vote Dilution." *University of San Francisco Law Review* 27(4):781–813.

Engstrom, Richard, and Michael McDonald. 1981. "The Election of Blacks to City Councils: Clarifying the Impact of Electoral Arrangements on the Seats–Population Relationship." *American Political Science Review* 75(2):344–54.

Guinier, Lani. 1991. "No Two Seats: The Elusive Quest for Political Equality." *Virginia Law Review* 77:1414–1514.

Guinier, Lani. 1994. *Tyranny of the Majority: Fundamental Fairness in Representative Democracy*. New York: Free Press.

Johnson, Richard. 1979. *Political, Electoral, and Spatial Systems*. Oxford: Oxford University Press.

Keech, William, and Michael Sistrom. 1994. "North Carolina." In *Quiet Revolution in the South: The Impact of the Voting Rights Act*, ed. Chandler Davidson and Bernard Grofman. Princeton: Princeton University Press.

Lakeman, Enid. 1970. *How Democracies Vote*. London: Faber and Faber.

Lijphart, Arend. 1994. *Electoral Systems and Party Systems*. New York: Oxford University Press.

Massey, Douglas, and Nancy Denton. 1987. "Trends in Residential Segregation of Blacks, Hispanics, and Asians: 1970–1980." *American Sociological Review* 52(6):802–25.

Pildes, Richard, and Kristen Donoghue. 1995. "Cumulative Voting in the United States." *University of Chicago Legal Forum*, 241–312.

Polinard, Jerry, Robert Wrinkle, and Tomas Longoria. 1991. "The Impact of District Elections on the Mexican American Community: The Electoral Perspective." *Social Science Quarterly* 72(3):608–14.

Sass, Tim R., and Stephen Mehay. N.d. "Minority Representation, Election Method, and Policy Influence." Department of Economics, Florida State University. Unpublished manuscript.

Still, Edward. 1984. "Alternatives to Single-Member Districts." In *Minority Vote Dilution*, ed. Chandler Davidson. Washington, DC: Howard University Press.

Still, Edward. 1991. "Voluntary Constituencies: Modified At-Large Voting as a Remedy for Minority Vote Dilution in Judicial Elections." *Yale Law and Policy Review* 9(2):354–69.

212   *Appendix B*

Swain, Carol. 1993. *Black Faces, Block Interests: The Representation of African-Americans in Congress*. Cambridge: Harvard University Press.

Taebel, Delbert. 1978. "Minority Representation on City Councils: The Impact of Structure on Blacks and Hispanics." *Social Science Quarterly* 59(1):142–52.

Thomas, James, and William Stewart. 1998. *Alabama Government and Politics*. Lincoln: University of Nebraska Press.

Vedlitz, Arnold, and Charles Johnson. 1982. "Community Segregation, Electoral Structure, and Minority Representation." *Social Science Quarterly* 63(4):729–36.

Welch, Susan. 1990. "The Impact of At-Large Elections on the Representation of Blacks and Hispanics." *Journal of Politics* 52(4):1050–76.

INDEX